Invisible Poets

Anthology 3

FUNDRAISING IN AID OF

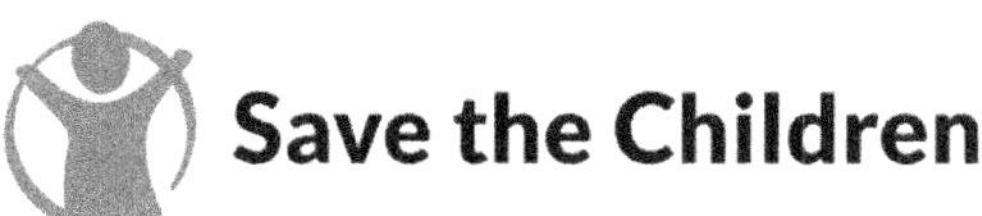

First published by
Wheelsong Books
United Kingdom

First published in 2025

Print ISBN: 9-798-30992-373-1

Contents

Foreword

This is the third Invisble Poets anthology. It is a collection of more than 240 poems—the result of a rigorous selection process. To be eligible for inclusion each poem had to be performed on *Live Poets Society*. Regular viewers will know that only the best poetry features on the show, which is broadcast live on the *Invisible Poets* Facebook group from the UK, the USA and other countries. The shows' presenters are all very knowledgeable about poetry, but they also have diverse tastes. As a result, the poetry in this anthology is diverse, with a wide variety of themes, styles and formats. That means there should be something for everyone within these pages.

Invisible Poets Anthologies 2 and 3 commemorate the second anniversary of Invisible Poets, which in its short life has gained a membership of more than 50,000 poets.

Your purchase of this anthology will not only benefit all the poets who are represented within these pages by gaining them a wider audience; it will also go a long way toward supporting children in crisis. Proceeds from the Amazon sales of this book will be donated to Save the Children—a worldwide relief fund that provides children in warzones and disaster areas with food, medicine, clothing, shelter—and eventually—education. It's a very worthy cause and we thank you for your valuable support.

Steve Wheeler
Poet and Founder
Invisible Poets and
Wheelsong Books

Muse Girl

Jamie Willis

With an ink well dip and finest tip
He crafted chaos to curation
He took a brushing wash
And passed across
My nuanced intimation
He saw the shadows and the hollows
Nestled next to the crescendos
Of my serpentine clandestine curves
And composition of my gossamer bones.
As if I were his creation.

To be the light of inspiration
And captured in the fascination
Of a diamond mind and master-crafting hands
Of one whose eye is stayed and fixed...
It's a mixture of both thrill and fear
To have his piercing scrutiny so near
To every shaded secret space...
But, development of shading
Is what sets apart the finest art.
So, graze my every willowed place...
And make sweet art of me.

If I had rested in a field of wildflowers
In resplendent sun-ray reach...
Or sauntered slow along the continental edge
Of fading summer's beach
Or danced in white alone at night
To Santana's stroking song...
He'd find a way to form it like tribute to a god.

He sees what he desires...
Does he see what's really there?
Are they the same, or do I even want to know—
Or do I even really care—

If art is imitating life
Am I this beautiful
Or is he just delusional...
Has he considered what he sees
May not even really be...

Either way, what he has done
Is craft my life into masterpiece.

Mapping Your Eyes

Fadi Yousef

I finally found you
An X on the map where our lips met
Having travelled forgotten names
Of mountains and valleys
And entitled countries
That romance can't pronounce
Over oceans and seas
Where my love almost drowned
As the waves inched me closer
To every mile in your blue eyes
To reach you in anonymous waters
Where you were down to your last breath
The map closing around you
As I put out a hand
Calming the creases
And we swam to the key in the corner
Coming to life in our own
Latitude and longitude
Where we folded our past
Using it for tinder in the fireplace
On an edgy night
Where we got to know each other better
Realizing the world
Is such a small place after all

Tobacco Times

Jason Horsler

They used to smoke on planes.
There were ashtrays built in trains
and the walls had yellow stains.

In all movie theatres too,
the flash of flint and then the hue—
every screen was coned in blue.

My grandad smoked in his car—
winter windows not ajar—
so we smelled like his cigar.

And my gran, with a squint and pout,
lit one up and stubbed one out;

gave her cigarette a tug
then dropped ash and, with a shrug,
said, 'it's good—good for the rug.'

Everything & Nothing

Archie Papa

Everything to accumulate and nothing to achieve
with volumes of gospel and nothing to believe
time bearing moments labored to conceive
youth lays to waste what age will grieve

Everything to wonder but nothing in thought
so much offered yet nothing was brought
wisdom shares what knowledge sought
dreaming of peace as wars are fought

Notions of Wonderment

Hahona Scribe

My notions of wonderment
are stars painting an infinite sky
My dreams are comets
illuminating the mercurial vastness
My tears are meteors
scorching my grasp of knowing
My footsteps take me to crossroads
which lead to enlightenment

Unyoked of marrowed bone
& carapace cocoon
I yield to kismets call
Moon shadows meld
as I take my totem form
In nocturnal relief
I cleave enchanting howls
Guttural howls
reverberatively regale
across the cosmos
in sacrosanct
teponaztli throng

Stardust bequeaths celestial maidens
These visions leave me spellbound
yet my knowing is thwarted
Within this corporeal embattlement
my soul summoned
as magnet to steel

So I must depart this reckoning
to fulfil my destiny
Traveling beyond the speed of light
the crescendo enraptures my being
The big bang propels this vessel
beyond the primordial ooze
beyond a minds incarceration

Released from mortal shackles
emancipated in spirit
at one with the creator
The easel of my creation
revealed in all its glory
my very blood & essence
etched upon the tablets of Zion
Genesis of enlightenment
Elysium!

the undefined heart

(of an unsigned book)

Matt Elmore

when falls a slight might, of ladylike light
sinking high above teenage dreams
as sleep calls night to draw starry heights
below mature realms of means

that I should ask, or seek that task
for reader now listen, look!
at wanton words unassured, unseen unheard
win the undefined heart of an unsigned book

how turning a page, pain plays on a stage
when a pleasure is less adored than read
how expressive a mage enclosed in a cage
the bleeding poet exposed concedes

which medium may, or technology say
what hidden feelings come to mean
or compassion felt under abuses' welt
need intimately become relieved

as classical verse serves a soft purse
causing pause in modern night
let sleep relieve dreams upon moonbeams
to rest easy for a new morning's flight

A Crystal Heart

Emile Pinet

Early Spring, fire and ice meld,
sculpting Winter into art.
And as shorter days lengthen
snowmen gain a crystal heart.

Nature dapples the landscape
with patches of green and white.
And migrating birds head home,
lured by the extended light.

Glistening on the rooftops,
gathering droplets, amass.
And dribbling down from the eaves
form icicles, clear as glass.

Disappearing instantly,
frosty breaths disperse to naught.
For such swirling contrails merge
with warm breezes, Spring has brought.

Invisible Poet

Craig Musso

I'm the invisible man
My words are neither seen nor heard.
It's as if the world suddenly went blind
or I've become something too dark to see.
If I write you a poem
and put it on here,
you would never know it
Just another invisible poet.

Plagiarist

Chuck Porretto

I don't write my words,
for I just see them floating by.
I know this sounds absurd
but they will often catch my eye.

If I force my sleeping pen
my words will fight me all the way,
but so every now and then
I find a floating word ballet.

They dance before by eyes
in what will seem to be a dare,
and then, to some surprise,
I've gone and plagiarized the air.

Static Symphony

Peter Rivers

In a world of stale notes, constant ears that are burning
Clumsy life sounds and melodies we are learning
Your failure echoes hum like a symphony
Your routine static has a buzz like a symphony
Your public displays of spite sound like a symphony
I do what I want kind of world,
All one man bands, no symphony
Everyone every country global pandemic
Psychotic screams, our gifted symphony
Is this all we are made of, is this our sweetest symphony?
This about it, how do you conduct your symphony?

Dark Tapestry—Grey Symphony

Iain Strachan

dark tapestry dark web
rotten in my brain
all the blackened unutterable
thoughts i dare not say
dare not articulate
to horrifying offensive language
writhing evil worms of ideas
of sinful hieroglyphics

dark tapestry of grey on black
floating like a pixelated Rothko
floatings of suppressed
misery and hatred
in the sewer of my sputtering
network of neurons and synapses
that passes for a mind

all the disgusting things
i might have said
tapping into the dark tapestry
dark web of my head
floating floating moving
slowly with the indistinct edges of
a grey symphony
sustained pianissimo drone

better not look too close
at those floating pixelated edges
and get sight of indescribable abominations
trigger chasms of churning anxiety
flooding from head to belly
twisting clenching unbearably
to vomit forth the last meal
but not the mental filth squirming

don't don't look at it it's really there
a rippling crapulent wasted blanket

devil's menu of shameful potentialities
all the might have been murderous thoughts
obsessive compulsive dread
of yielding to violence
of acts of dreams
of the extremes of screams
of rotting syllables of all the thoughts
you really don't want to think

let them settle
or maybe hold up the filthy rotten disgusting thing
against the light and dimly slowly observe
the emergence of white flecks
through the tatty warp and weft
of the black fabric
indistinct the pattern at first
but concentrate resolve no longer
to be magnetized
by the chaos of this evil purulent tapestry
focus the white lights to
constellations patterns anything
to create a meaning like the stars were seen
as heroes, giant animals, anything
to make a cluster of metaphors legends myths
to create your own framework
your own system of survival of thrival

now put the thing down; you've aired it
let go of some of the stink
no longer scared of it
the vile chasm of crappy chatter
turns to the music of life
and the grey symphony
slowly acquires vibrant colours

the depression has lifted
the panic attack lapsed
the urge to vomit vanished
ready again to gorge
on the lovely fruits of life.

Dream 2

Andy Reay

Lifting the shadows of porcupine heat
Along the passageway grandfathers replete
Shattered and folded a ring for your finger
Wrinkled hands and nicotine stains linger
Colossal dust engrained in skin
Burns like a beetle held tight within
A circus of flies flying and leaping
Animals howl and singers keep singing
A Turkish tomato sits on your plate
All alone crying and selling you late
Hundreds of tigers looking, growling
Cute little piggies frightened, howling
a tortured tattoo growls on your arm
it will not hurt, no need for alarm
sixty singers sifting through dirt
and a glass eyed eagle is on high alert
a shadow-man hidden down a dark path
a young woman laughing her last laugh
tearful tarantulas hide in a corner
they could bite, but nobody warned ya
now each and every one you can see
stand in line, waiting for a taxi

Random Sound Bite #1

Steve Wheeler

Break the silence
Tell me the truth
Bring the flair to life
Not quite as silky smooth
A perfect mish-mash
The flames that rise
Show me the cash
Your guests have arrived

End of Day

Terry Bridges

A calmness extends...a vast level beach
No unexploded bombs to detonate my fury
This still evening beyond the tempest' s reach
It soothes like a medicine...no fuss no hurry

I tarry in the sweet afterglow of day
Linger among the rock-pools and ebbing tide
What is to come...a concern from yesterday
Forgotten in these nuances that abide

Detail upon detail drawn in the summer strand
I will remember each whisper of the breeze
Worries collapse...washed away like castles of sand
The mighty empire of death brought to its knees

This triumph of arching rainbow over the sea
As cool twilight unfolds its silent canopy

A Coalescence of Sparks

Emile Pinet

The manifestation of God's word,
The Big Bang created the universe,
a phantasmagorical coalescence of sparks.

Billions of galaxies swirl in the fabric of time and space
like filigree clusters set with pulsars and quasars,
and massive black holes generating cosmic rays.

Stewards of both life and death, stars define infinity;
as black matter anchors gravity's web of threads
blurring boundaries of science and creation,
life floats in an unfathomable sea of ebony.

Kundalini Airport

Kate Cameron

Paco takes his harmonica
wild as the Arabian Sea
hissing below
blown in white horses
sparkling with snow

as wild as birdsong snaking a soul
Shiva on the rocks in cannabis smug
patchouli anthems pulling sands
searing heat another land

You sit and smoke
in a Buddhic way,
I am mesmerised
and dance and sway,
as the vibrant market
is packed away

on damp palm leaf floor
I saw her dance, alone
sublimely tranced
pale blond, loose hair
waxy flowers entwined
face rosy in the heat

a foreign apparition
as the sitar rose
to implore
dreamlike naive being—she
caught in evening light

on this wild & rakish coast
with its flocks of eagles
and drunk mosquitos
far east of Eden

I Write for a Summer Flower

Rafik Romdhani

I don't write for peacocks
relishing in lush shadows,
seeing nothing except
their own colours.
I don't write for croaking frogs
busy with their greenish ponds.
No, I don't for they would hear nothing
from my crashing words.
I don't write for wind-blown coats
and fear-sharpened legs.
I don't write for ghosts
in their visualized forests.
I write for a summer flower
having survived all the fires.
I grapple with time's splinters
on erupting eyes and determined
faces standing still like grey gods.
I write to get drunk from my own words.

Do Not Waver

Andy Reay

Her wine glass half full
While mine remains
miserably half empty
She smiles, plans gushing
I just sit and wait for my exclusion,
the normal course of things
Her smile, her gaze though,
does not waver
She hears my nervous laughter
And feels myself doubt

"Do not worry, nor waver,
I have you and you have me now"
I look into her eyes, and see this is true

On Wings of Faith

Trude Foster

Today I set my pages free
scattered wide, and apart from me
for months, no years, I have held them true
close to my chest as they blossomed and grew
when I opened my arms, away they flew
I could not keep them, they wanted to go
It was only fair, but I wish it were not so

August 3rd

Aoife Cunningham

He passed this morning
without warning
it wasn't alarming
For decades
addiction feasted upon his will
left behind a carcass of missed milestones.
He stopped breathing on a bed of roses,
memory petals and the thorns of mistake
pricked his skin, he bled remorse.
Finally free from the flames of fixation.

Insecticide

David Simpson

Louise ate ants and frogs and things,
Crawly spiders and bugs with wings,
Wiggly worms and garden snails,
Crunchy slaters and dragonfly tails.

Her mother at first was worried,
But now she beams with pride,
Because her lovely daughter,
Is an effective insecticide.

A Different Crown

James Hurst

I see my reflection in a window pane
Face looks happy but not the same
A former shadow and because
Life's not been kind and what is now was
Day to day going through the motions
Face strained and no emotions
How can I continue thus
As life remains a succubus
And as I wake up everyday
Obstacles get in my way
Surely it should not be this hard
But life has no boundaries and will disregard
Any attempt to get on top
These altercations do not stop
So life it has a different path for me
It does not want me to be free
Seems like it wants my life to fail
Falter and not prevail
But I have a different track
One where I will fight back
One where I will stand up and say
That I am strong and here to stay
And I will wear a different crown
Life will not get me down

Random Sound Bite #2

Steve Wheeler

I stand at an angle to the world
It's just like stepping back in time
I'm not thirsty for money,
but I have a hunger for art

Front Porch Memories

John David Meadows

I'm sitting on the same front porch
My grandma and grandpa did
I can almost see them both right now
And hear the things they said.

I can see grandma snapping beans
We picked earlier in the day
And see grandad in the swing
As back and forth he'd sway.

On a day humid and cloudy
Much like it is this day
Reminders are all around me
And I like it that way.

It makes it so easy to go back in time
When I want to write and reminisce
Thanking God for the memories that are mine
Of those I've loved and miss.

For Evermore

Sean D. Timms

Breeze echoes and ghostly tides
grassy moorlands and mountainous plateaus
Red kites crying within the windy blue ride
Elegiac and sacred like the dying vista
Suns dying rays their faces amber
Streamlined hums of liquid gurgles
A tenebrous spanse of dragons breath
Sweeping grandeur across the natural beauty
manifesting itself as a welcoming cuutch
Grey jagged crags on hilltops clamber
Hikers ramblers and abseilers gather
Interest peaked by natures beauty
As Brecon's Beacon lives

Windows

Gregory Richard Barden

look …

look close, my gaze
the shine of what endures …
can you not see the toil of my father—
the glint of my mother's care?
do the joys of childhood and the
ache of young loves, lost
not shimmer in those depths?

look, yet, my eyes
beyond the white and absinthe
plunge those oily, breathless blacks ...
a brand dances there, yet
flickering for the dreams not realized
the lone, weary heart unwanted
and the songs ...

unsung.

Poet

Tim Queen

all the good words
fall thru the hole
in Frank's pocket.

he gathers them
arranges randomly
they make too much sense.

he burns them in the
backyard.

This is You

Nwafor Amarachi Grace

A mighty mortal,
Destined for greatness
An invisible storm
That scares other storms
A fearless David
That killed Goliath
A strong Samson
That brought down a whole city
An Esther with a unique heart
A heart full of love
A wise Solomon
With unlimited riches
An age grade Methuselah
The oldest man on earth
The best of the bests
A stronghold no one can bring down.

When Days Entwine

Neil Forsyth

Lost on the horizon of a lonely sea
As wind and rain combines
Going nowhere aimlessly
Yet the morning sun still shines

Lost in adventure in this life
God knows what's in store
Each page you turn, each moment rife
Just leaves you wanting more

whispers

Bardin Boyd

i'm supposed to be whole
but all i am is a fraction
i try to add love
but all i get is subtraction
i wanna multiply
but all i get is division
i try be an exponent
but i'm not a mathematician

i watch life creep away
the sun sinks, times go by
they say that i'm broken
the pen drips
the heart cries

people watch
—waiting for me to die—
shouting hello,
then
whispering goodbye

Bleed

Tom Cleary

Love is a thorn.
Shorn of my flesh
I am defenceless.
It carves a niche
to bleed
a delicate watercolor
without boundaries.

Unmystic Fear

Kate Cameron

Lady Lazarus walked the line
prismatically broken
as refracted sunshine
dreaming of my father's yellow vine,
bitter pilgrim grapes
were mine

Byzantine image—entombed in the lake
the gold that gleamed dully
would never escape

tragic ballerina roses softly shed
ruffled petals for some gods bed
offered me an apple as the moment bled
Lyrical summer burned to red

my evasive calligraphy of downy flames
rich glowing saffron and light laced rose
casting a magic lantern show
hides scarring emotions as fallen snow

flying creature clutches at asphalt runways
unmystic fear in sapphire eyes
heavy stone tongue embossed with lead
veiled bowed head

your fugitive divinity
casts a mottled white wing
flawed as dawnlit darkness wings
far away inky night
lit by smouldering gorse fires
desiring evasive flight

and then there was power
and then there was light

Without the Impediment of Experience

Mike Absalom

Tap tap went my cane.
A woman approached me on the road.
"Are you a nurse?" I asked.
She walked with me through hill and field;
not right nor left, not up and down,
but simply within the unworldly dimensions of a poem.

"You must be a nurse," I said.
"No one comes here, except to minister to the fading away."
Tap tap tap went my cane.
"Although," I added, as an afterthought,
noticing the red cross on her breast,
"If you are a Crusader, you are too late."

Then, and without the impediment of experience
I thought it tactful to switch channels.

The gap-toothed larches, bearded for winter,
grin out from the edge of the Evergreen Woods.
I pass a black stallion,
its coat burred with sunlight,
facing away to the east,
snorting.
An Arab bloodline, I saw clearly,
pulsing with the future.
Poised,
within the worldly dimensions of a religion.

I am alone now. I go
like a spun-glass caterpillar in the morning light.
And the rain begins,
slowly,
raising nipples on the puddles.

I smile to myself.
Without the impediment of experience
it is easy.

Summer Baptism

Helen Laycock

You flinch
at the cold
of the first drops,

at the shatter
of soft glass
on the tilt of your face.

But skywater
gloriously rakes
your lashes
and parts your hair,

its fingers
finding their way
inside
your shirt,

draping you bare,

and you open your mouth,
tongue-taste
its tin kiss,

your neck
a trickling bridge
beyond which
mind and body
have

floated
away.

One Long and Windy Night
Martin Gedge

Looking out my window on one long and windy night
When I noticed of a shadow that reflected candle light
Of a girl who stood there crying against a glass of shattered pain
As to wonder to the reason there was treason in the rain
I could tell her heart was broken as she was choking on her tears
No longer made of flowers breaking showers on her fears
I could feel a bit of tension apprehension in the cold
Escaped out from the fire with the desire to unfold
And to have lost of all that smile just for a while standing there
I couldn't help but tender her surrender in the air
And from a drawn out curtain being certain she would see
Another broken shadow who would share her company
Like a whisper on the wind so taken in I had to know
Was it all just make believe should I just leave and let her go
And deep out in the distance with persistence of the storm
To my surprise those midnight eyes would rise in size and form
An entity so close to me a ghost to freely roam
That once inside this girl had died to hide inside this home
One touch with death one spoken breath still left here I remain
Out from a dream awake to scream to steam my window pane.

Lonely
neil mason

i wandered lonely as a cloud
but not as lonely as John Tracy in Thunderbird 5
never seeing a soul for months on end
lonely as a single sock devoured
by the washing machine gremlins
no soul mate to kick around with
the last sweet in the tin at Christmas time
a lonely toffee stuck inside a paper wrapper prison
not an ideal way for anyone to be
i pray that good people will never be lonely

Hypnagogic

Terry Bridges

A thud in my ear
Announcing trouble
Some cat is going wild
Searching out victims
Suicides and deadbeats
The dumb sound of despair

Is there anyone there?
I can hear them knocking
Insanely...vamoose!
Of all the damned times
To be serenading
This city is frightening

Noise scrapes chalk on blackboard
Searching rising tension
A finger-nail sketch
Of ultimate terror
The nervous system
In shock and horror

Cowering under sheets
Gibbering...afraid to move
The dead hour motionless
Will it ever end?
This silent nocturne
Wheels within wheels

Thinking lying awake
Sleepless but OK.

Coda: written straight
off in 10 minutes.
Then stopped.

write yourself down

Chuck Porretto

write yourself down
and write yourself out
write what you found
while digging about

write it all down
whisper or shout
before it is bound
by a bottleneck bout

write yourself down
yes spill it all out
like rain on the ground
right after a drought

just write it all down
then drain it all out
a dawdler may drown
in an ocean of doubt

just write yourself down

Sticks and Stones

El Bardd

Sticks and Stones they threw at us...
And we picked up every piece

Now when it rains,
they pay for the sticks to build a fire...
And when the sun becomes unbearable,
they pay for the stones to build their homes.

Moonlight

Sarah Wheatley-Tillbrook

When the moon did find its virtue
Upon an unlit path
A line where lay its worth
As with it, much fear did pass
I too found recollection
Of my inner higher light
Shines in my own direction
To light the darkest night
For all much have a brightness
As all must hold its grey
And to summer in this insight
Is to create better days
So reach out That spark within you
The part that makes you, unique
For what makes you individual
Is what lights the path we seek

Succumb

Brandon Adam Haven

Drowning within a thousand waves of void,
I wail for help, smitten with empty woe.
My cries go unheard, my soul destroyed.
I've always had to deal with suffering alone.

Lost in voyage with a sedated susurrous tongue,
Speaking a meaningless language, quick to be silenced.
Succumbing to the bleak mythos of an empty lung,
All peace now ephemeral beyond the consciousness of violence.

Drowning in waste, succinctly succumbing,
Pulling the trigger to put an end to rampant thoughts running.
For freedom lies under a cold, blossomed decay,
Or cremated with ashes flown so far away.

Slavic Pizzazz

Iain Strachan

I fizz up my life with Slavic pizzazz—
dances by Dvorak with Czechian glaze—
Brash celebration and razzamatazz.

A Russian composer who loved to jazz
Shostakovich's polkas that set them ablaze,
so, fizz up your life with Slavic pizzazz.

Open a bottle of spicy Shiraz
Or drink twenty vodkas and end in a daze
Of brash celebration and razzamatazz.

Put on your jewels of jade and topaz—
Gemstones from Russia and start off a craze
So, fizz up your life with Slavic pizzazz.

Doing the sword dance, as dangerous az
the whips of a blade that can maim or graze;
a brash celebration and razzamatazz.

Put on Czeched clothes and endeavour to snazz
up your wardrobe to dazzle, amaze
and fizz up your life with Slavic pizzazz.
Make brash celebration and razzamatazz.

Grape

David Simpson

I took a grape out to lunch,
What the hell, I took a bunch,
Not in their shiny skins so tight,
But in a bottle, as you might.

Mowing them Down

Ryan Morgan

Cut the lawn
With the severe machine,
Severing organic insurgence
In pursuit of order.
Yellow blooms
With mustardy plumes
From the clover carpet.
Little knots of blue
Brocade its tufted epaulettes
And skeletal stalks of dandelion clocks
Poke out of the ground
Their payload long exhausted,
Like the butterflies which flap
Tiredly among the blades
Listless biplanes low on fuel.
There is a growing army
Of wild grass spears,
Irregulars on the field,
Arrayed against the nettle hordes
Accompanying the medical corps
Of hunkering dock leaves.
It's a wondrous confusion of life,
A chaos of mixed metaphor.
And it all had to go
Scythed to stubble
Under the wheels of my vision.
After, I survey the butcher's bill.
All is neat, close cropped.
An army cut in uniform green.
There's satisfaction in the ordering
But not much joy.

A Tree at the Bank

Rafik Romdhani

I almost became a tree at the bank.
I have grown roots and green veins
on both temples.
The crooked queue that rose
before the sun consisted of
boiling heads and tired faces.
The only cashier comes in, sits down
and mumbles as if he were not here.
Many irked eyes are on wristwatches,
waiting for their turn.
All the trees in the line wish to be
uprooted, to even disappear.
The stifling space started to feel like a bier
as I scowled and scowled on the cashier.
Half the day was literally gone.
The crooked queue groans.
I have grown roots and green veins
on both temples.
I almost became a tree from standing here.

Sleep

(Double Acrostic)

by Archie Papa

Softening the edges of the abyss
let the chaos of time pass over the soul
each of us will venture here alone
every dream will offer something true
precious moments gathered while we sleep

The Love in Your Eyes

Janet Tai

Every evening
When your work
Is done for the day
You walk into the house
Via the kitchen.
I would be busy
Prepping dinner but a smile
For you is a must.
In return you look at me
With those irresistible eyes
To land a kiss on my lips.
You smell of
Grease and grime but who cares?
Your loving kisses are so worth it.

Mesmerizing

Nan DeNoy'er

Music it set the rhythm
tempo ignited their soul
into a burning flame
it consumed them beyond
into another dimension.

It drew them to embrace
its mesmerizing movement
capturing the soul
into their web of disguise
desire with no return.

Intriguing the beat
Tantalizing it was as
they danced entwined
magical was the moment
they transcended time and space.

Poet-Gymnasts

Terry Bridges

To live high in the ethereal sky
Bouncing energy off the sun
Supernova fun a spectacular show
Theatrical performing trapeze-artistes
Screaming through the teeth of heavy air
Dangers everywhere you look beware
The attractions of being still will tempt
Treat quiet with contempt and wild laughter
After the gold rush reckon the debit
Credit each loss of coward reticence
There is sense in exceeding limits and slow patience
Dim-wit speedos beat extinct dodos
Who comprehends the fate of sparrows and robins
Tumbling off their narrow perches stone dead
Here lie those whose names are unrecorded

Diviner

Linda Adelia Powers

Slipstream of the ambivalent
Ambient chorus of shifting ambitions
Subliminal moons rising into the clouds
Prancing like sparks in the shallows

Motionless spirals of dreamless sleep
Skyscrapers of memory frozen
Cliffs collapsing in one breath of time
Suns rampant erasing the sky

Kinetic shades diffused from beyond
Dispersal of stories ancient anew
Heads doused with shimmering haloes of dew
Oracles whispering names of the few

Free

Gemma Tansey

I think it's finally happening
I'm freeing myself from these chains
I've wrestled with a demon from hell
and now love is all that remains

Hindsight gifted me insight
As I wrestled through the mess
Killed the trauma that wasn't mine
And decided it's not worth the stress

I realised an awful lot
That mainly I'm harming me
All that dissonance was making me ill
And it stemmed from not wanting to see

I had to venture deep within
And comfort my inner child
Face both the dark as well as light
And my heart is now reconciled

Now I know I'm worthy & strong
After a month of introspection
I was never broken or off my head
I just needed my own affection

The universe is sending me signs
And I know I'm on the right track
I've left the pain and found the magic
And now there is no looking back

Paint the Whole World

Andy Reay

Paint my love for you
For all the years of joining
Paint the struggles, the sacrifice
The laughter, the joy

Paint my sadness, my grief
At souls never again to speak
And paint me as I wipe your tears
For pain and sadness belong to both

Paint our summer days
Picnics by the sea, a light breeze
Hands held as we follow the shore
Yes, please paint those days

And paint the day's end
As we sit in twilight years
Your head against mine,
as you paint grey upon grey

Paint the oranges and yellows above
And the trees, now in silhouette
Paint the whole world my love
So that I too can see

Random Sound Bite #3

Steve Wheeler

Spoon fed life
Couch potato life
Neurotic narcotic
Wasted life
Wasted opportunities
Wasted years

Sunday Dad

Olivia Knotts

The beep-beeping machine drills into every brain,
The orange haired clown that mocks the insane.
Amid the cartons, straws and screaming kids
I try to stay contained, closing my lids.
You see, I spotted amid the mindless bores
and gnashing Jaws, the one alone that remained.
In a space that feels detached, remote and collapsed,
I continue to remain restrained.

Fresh murals on doors, greasy patterned floors—
Who has the largest fry?
I noticed..
brown eyes didn't, I watched her blubber and cry.
The Sunday Dads, with their midweek
almost-forgotten girls and lads,
Desperately letting time pass,
never admitting they are bored to the bone
Each of them glancing for a second to check
then fixing their eyes swiftly back on their phone

Always a Happy Meal or some plasticized deal
Nothing in this place ever look close to real

But it keeps the children quiet for a while
as per the Maccy D style
Each of their faces adorned
with a media-washed, flaky smile.
A waif with greasy hair, adrift, unfitting within the glut,
rubbish and meaningless rubble,
Filthy jeans—bet she never ate her greens,
the AC/DC on her T hints of trouble.
Five sugars poured into her Coke,
rolling her eyes at the ogling detached dads
What a joke

"Come on, come on now," that patty never saw a cow,
Limp lettuce in a dry bap, watching the woman

collecting trays in her logo-stamped cap,
Waddling in black trousers past each
stuck down chair and table—haha no,
no way... could you liken her to a Betty Grable.

But this lanky, unfitting seemingly lonely girl,
With her pasty skin—
I know...
There's something about her, not outward,
but observable from within.
As she stands and looks towards the door—
As the world keeps spinning, she's is waiting
Patiently wanting something more.

Beyond

Imelda Zapata Garcia

Across the universe
beyond realms where yearning
sits on burgeoning flame
there stirs fledgling flutter
of sounds in silence uttered
reverberating just the same
There, go failing promises
of peaceful slumber
we toil away long hours
to seize a setting sun in frame
in hopes of reaching summits
as sand of time yet plummets
in this game
Where Oceans birth leviathans
to hold our breath
upon the sight of grandeur
dwarfing steps we take
Hence imparting nuance
songs of Sirens of the notion
we've achieved a breadth
golden gates we thought to break

Our Run

Becky Topham

We run—synchronised—
Upon the sunset's red
Through the gnarled trees
Past the flower beds

Our breath escapes
In plumes of white
Already promising
An icy night

There is crunching
Beneath our pounding feet—
Below freezing now
But neither acknowledge defeat

I glance at you
At the pinkness of your face—
And I pretend that your life
Did not go to waste

And I think:
"How could it ever be—
That I no longer have you,
And you no longer have me?"

Then I berate myself
This is all an illusion
That you run beside me
A grief filled delusion

And yet, here you are
Weaving through the trees
Skeletal now
Robbed of their leaves

We laugh breathless
Almost as one
Only then do I remind myself
That my twin is gone

bow

Ayub Babikir

now I awake
to a riot of roosters, their crows
stinging this young air
like red stars,
to the clouds layered
in rows like a stack of dishes.
and the faint half-moon
wavering, like an Imam's hat
in the wind.

the tree in our yard, our constant dancer
is now still, in awe.
as she, like me, is taken
by this gift of a morning.
she seems to bow, to shrink
as do the walls and poles and me, knowing
that the space we yield
will be claimed
by something beautiful, something
more than us.

and so we bow,
gladly
bow . . .

My Hue

Aoife Cunningham

my hue
is green and blue.
Spirited saintly sometimes
with a smudge of me
and a smear of you
turquoise in our eye

Ocean Heart

Peter Rimmer

Rain torrents
From the heart of a dark sky
This land is water plump
Astonishingly green.

Sunlight comes hard through cloud breaks
Caressing skin with a warm embrace
August knows how to break hearts
And raise hopes in the space
Of an eyeblink.

Illusions are shattered
As sky opens its ocean heart
This benediction of cold comfort
Dousing any thoughts of warm languor
August is the month that will let you down
With a smile, a rakish bounce to its stride
Stealing light from the night in lengthening days.

Dark as the Captain

Trude Foster

Dylan boy,
lord of all the sleeping towns
the valleys and the mean little houses,
master of the flowering words,
like best bitter they flowed
dark and ripe and full to the top of the glass,
well worth the waiting for you were,
if the masses couldn't see it
then they too were blind as moles,
you finished up your pint
and left us, empty

Fragrant Memory

Marie Harris

Against a fading brick wall
In the garden of her memories
A flower of passionate red
Bled the color of her emptiness
Closing her eyes she felt yesterday
Lifting her from this moment in time
Taking her back to his loving embrace
His tender kiss upon her lips
His touch so warm and familiar
His essence lingering
A breeze softly nudged her reverie
Reminding her that he was gone
A split in space and the mercurial whimsy
Of fate and the separation of heart and soul
She was drifting like a wind tossed petal
From her favorite flower as it bloomed beautifully
The fragrance wafting, filling her senses with
An aroma of forever, perfuming her loneliness
Inhaling the scented memories she succumbed
To the silent fall of a glistening tear
As it travelled the contours of her face
Landing on her outstretched hand
Reaching for yesterday
She laid her cheek against the fading stone
And whispered to the descending night
Cover me within your shade of darkness
There, let his memory hold me
Then let him kiss me softly
And bid me a sweet goodnight
While the fragrance from the garden
Wraps us in love's embrace

Writing Brings Me Back

Natasha Browne

Do you ever notice
That writing brings you to that place,
Where a memory is stored,
In your hemisphere,
Back to a place,
When you felt at lost,
Or inspired to write,
To ignite,
A flicker of a flame,
Not seeking fortune or fame,
Writing to keep sane,
Not sharing your work,
When nobody knew your name,
I came here,
To write,
To shed some light,
On my many past grievances
Harrowing deep into my core,
Where I always wanted somewhat more,
To explore the confines of my mind,
Shedding those underlying lines,
Where it was just me,
Writing poetry,
Not willing to share,
In the thought no-one cared,
What I had to say,
Just me writing night and day,
Writing brings me back,
To that place I thought I lacked,
Something in between,
When my story was unseen,
In a place I'd never been,
Where my sane thoughts were intact,
writing brings me back.

Hive Music

Ryan Morgan

The humming bee orchestra
Play a symphony amidst the blooms' scent,
Hunting furiously for nectar
In a harmoniously concerted movement.
The murmuring of their industrious wings
Throng blossoms with a bouquet of sound,
Like soaring strains of violin strings
In a floral auditorium's gay surround.
Each player knows their line by instinct
Every entry perfectly timed
The weaving counterpoint is exquisite
As their melodies entwine.
Their dulcet strains are euphoric:
Pulses of nature which resonate.
The music they make is hypnotic,
Lulling the listener into a fugue state.
There is no visible conductor
For this ensemble of apiary virtuosity,
Is there an invisible composer
Who scores fugal bee euphony?

Seraphic Sheddings

Brandon Adam Haven

Stricken in awe,
I behold the helm of beauty's plight.
Nestled by the sweet ambrosia of her soft lips,
Billowed beneath the veil of an audacious light—
This bright, seraphic shedding my worn armoire;

Her glow folds my heart into a thousand ethers,
Where I shine beyond despair and wail.
Her soft solace, tattered in unwinding tethers,
Her majestic wind soothing my tired sail.
Alas, this piercing aura haunts me forever.

Grand Finale

Dave Catterton Grantz

When I push on beyond my fetters
Of timely matters, beyond delusion,
And chill of space confounds confusion,
I'll not shiver without my shoes on,
And no, I'll not need my sweaters.

If my spirit be allowed to roam,
I'll circle back astride sunrise;
And if I be blessed with sighted eyes,
I'll feast them through the cobalt skies
Where Gaian winds blow flesh on bone.

My ears risen from the chanting surf,
My nostrils flared like a dancing horse,
I'll drink my fill without remorse,
And then I'll focus upon the source
Of life for me, back to my birth,

Where parents, dear, held me, swaddled,
As brother-sisters pranced around,
Fallen out from time's puffed gown,
Twisting skyward without a sound,
Freed from garments we had tottled.

Then off I'll be to see my Sharron,
Our daughters, dear, sprung from our clay,
Then *their* children, precious, out at play,
And for the grand finale of this day,
I'll summon all my love and caring,

And as I spiral above the sea,
I'll embrace it all, eternally.

Twice Mine

Jason Horsler

The boat was longer than his arm;
it was taller than his knee;
and he set it on the lake
to watch it sailing far and free.
it had taken him all winter
to shape and sand the wood.

He sewed and rigged the sail
and decided it was good.
Now an errant wind came foul
and blew it beyond and gone,
so the boy went home in sorrow
to mourn its passing on.

Then weeks and weeks went by
and the boy, in town one day,
gasped with joy to see his boat
in a shop window display.

Someone had walked along the shore
and come across his toy
and sold it to the shopkeeper.

So, in love, this creative boy
ran home to gather all his coin
to buy his own boat back
and when he did, he fixed its spars
so it could run and tack.

New painted and now attached
to his hand by a long strong line.
"I made you and now I've bought you—
forever you are twice mine."

Conflagration in Cumulus

Peter Rivers

This sky of blazing fire, a sure sign that times are dire
From up here I swear I even see the gossip
On the telephone wire
What kind of trash can we talk?

We live in painted boxes, mine sure looks
Painted with periwinkle chalk.
I think it stands out, other people talk smack
I hear them while they walk

Did you hear about the chimney sweep
That broke his back on that roof so steep?
Poor guy drives a rusted out Jeep,
With no work I bet that's a car hard to upkeep.
I mean that thing has so much rust
If it got in an accident it might turn to dust!

How about that frisky family, I think they have forty cats!
One thing is for sure, I doubt they have a problem with rats...
Is it weird that when I see them
Instead of hello I wanna say mew mew?
Don't even lie, you'd wanna do that too!

I find it totally cool, there are lessons in the world
You don't learn in a school
What makes the clouds turn into flames?
I'm sure every bright person
Has some scientific reasoning logic blames
These are the random things
That have the most power to inspire
You know you've found one when mere minutes
Transforms into an hour

This is just the proof, the sun is a dragon,
Now watch it breath fire...

Change

Ayub Babikir

the sun had just risen, and yet
how old
the day feels already,
how in the moments that drag themselves
in a row of tired breaths, a thin skin
can be heard tearing.

in the cup of tea waiting in front of me,
with the somber uninterest of a horse that
never knew a day of health, I see
the failed predictions
of an ancient diviner,
and yet these lies
now awaken, these undead specters
of a nameless charlatan.

the wind of this morning,
it can be gentle
on this groaning mass on whose shoulders
it rides,
it can be a light kiss
on this dying forehead,
but the wind is young, and the young
are seldom merciful.
it gnaws on this morning, this wind
of change,
in its quiet hum you can hear teeth
go into easy flesh,
you can see the light in the east
grow fainter,
you can taste the bitter breaths of malaria
on the roses,
and the streets

get a new crack every heartbeat or so
it could be gentle, this wind...

but change
is not the delicate fawn
but her predator...

A Splendour of Colour

Martin Gedge

A walk among a wondrous world of colorescent view
In pearls of prize its braising eyes of sweat palmetto dew
To wake the morn all fresh and born to form its blush parade
A forest saint of hue and paint as quaint as heaven made
To web its weave of magic seed to bleed and feed the air
Of fire burn to often churn to earn the fall affair
As cool the rain through autumn vein
Of flame and puddled ground
In fields of glow to often show each row of pumpkin town
And cheer of fest onto its guest to rest the best at heart
A splendor craft of nature's path to graph a moments start
As starry night so bold and bright to light the evening sky
You wish a star as high and far to jar this firefly
On whispering winds as mother
Spins her fins around the trees
To flutter dance a sweet romance each branch until its leaves
To feel a chill to often spill the will of all its charms
As far and wide this wild ride with pride and open arms
For better of this weather wear your sweater comfort care
Beneath the moon this garden bloom
With so much room to share
A breath so deep of precious keep of sounding sleep and taste
It's nature's way as seasons play to pray with love and grace ...

A New Day

Tom Watkins

The silence
of the crashing waves
pulls the sun
from the ocean floor
to illuminate a new day,
a new beginning
for the entire world

Slowly the waves
erase yesterday's footsteps
A fresh palette
for us to paint is created
The possibilities are as endless
as our collective imaginations

This morning
opened my eyes early
to this day
The rising sun warms me
as I embrace the possibles

A new day has risen
elevating tranquil hope

Echo

David Cragg

This sadness is just an echo of the past
And it will be gone by morn
Evaporated as mist when touched by kind light
Receding into nothing as mysteriously as it came
Leaving our true selves shining

Wheel Spins

Charlene Phare

For every car that backfires
And every bike bell that rings
There's method in the madness
As Saturn spins her rings

When answers remain hidden
And connectivity poor
There's nothing to console you
As you can't take anymore

When setting wheels in motion
And time to bring the changes
There's knowledge that you cling to
As your new gear engages

You're driving with conviction
Revelling in the power
Overtaking in the slow lanes
Extracting sweet from sour

The Unquenchable Fire

Stephen W. Atkinson

9/11
The towers fell, and the world changed
And so began the great exchange
Of hate
Of lies
Of family ties
Severed at the soul of man
For what? Allah's master plan?
There was no god on that bleak day
Only man's abuse of a belief astray
The dust still gathers; our lungs still choked
As we try to escape from the fire stoked.

Alone in My Mind

Gavin Prinsloo

You cannot go to that place where poets find peace,
or experience the sweet release
from the bondage of the status quo;
nor could you discover the dreams that only poets know.

A dreamer am I and by and by
it changes my state of perplexed wonder,
and tears asunder the fabric that held me blind,
opening the mind to awaken the imaginings that it may find.

I stand alone with neither sticks nor stones
and hold my silence where judgement is due but not for you,
oh no not for you, a man of verses,
for to judge is to render unto deed violence and vile curses.

Alone I stand in a mind of sand forever shifting,
words gliding and sliding, meaning hiding,
that can only exist when quill meets paper,
words vapour slipping where poets persist,
and their shadows linger and fade,
dissolving into the verses they've made.

I am alone in my mind, you cannot hear my voice,
it is by choice that I perpetuate the illusion
and perpetrate the inflictions that I find within,
bound by sin yet absolved by madness, bound by sadness,
a place, a place where stories begin.

The Lie of the Love (The Kiss)

Wayne Riley

She held me close to her chest
And I could feel her warm breath on my neck,
Still her arms,
Which were wrapped tightly around me
Somehow kept me away.
And then she told me that she loved me.
"I love you too," I told her,
And wished that I did.

Her love liberates the lips
Just as surely as the eyes deny the heart.
And the kiss,
Complete in its fullness
Left me empty and alone.
I accept now that I am no longer able to feel love.
That I feel anything at all is a trick of the mind.
I close my eyes and death comes in the form of sleep,
It won't last long though—
It never does..

The Ghost of Yesterday

Lorna McLaren

Can you see me, do I exist
or am I just a fading mist
that once was loved and now unseen,
a memory of what I once had been?
Can you hear me or do I have no voice,
is what I say just static noise
when once my words you thought so sweet
now go unheard as they deplete?
A fleeting memory of what's gone before,
lost to time and are no more,
unseen, unheard I drift away,
I am the ghost of yesterday!

Sunset on My Way Back Home

Kayla Ethan

Work, roads, jams, crowds
Daily scripts of my existence
Sleepless hours, tired eyes, aching body
Oh... let me get lost in dreamland.

When the sky spills its drowsy palette
That's when I know I've wrapped up a day
Behind the wheel, car engine humming
Driving towards home.

I put on some music
"Oh, I want something just like this..."
I sing along with Coldplay
Window down, fresh breeze embracing.

Then I catch sight of it
The sun dipping low, painting skies anew
A canvas of hues where day meets dusk
Trees dancing gently in silhouette.

I stop for a while to capture this moment.
A reminder laid before me
Of hope and beauty we find in the simplest moments
In every sunset, new stories will appear
A promise of new beginnings.

Cycle of life
To tire
To shoulder burdens
To feel joy through nature's kindness
Always revealed to me
Everything in its own time.

Resurrected Poets

Gavin Prinsloo

Would you know if the Devil were Poe,
  resurrected and born again?
Would that ravens call from beyond the wall
  that separates life from pain?

Would Longfellow lay his head upon the pillows of the dead,
  in houses plagued with ill?
Would Shakespeare shiver and upon a verse deliver,
  words not of his will?

Would Plath defy eternal wrath
  toward those who ended their own pain?
A thousand times writing the same screaming lines,
  has she lived would she do it again?

Would Annabelle speak and was Frost too weak
  to let death sunder loves grace?
Could she arise under deaths cold eyes
  for him to gaze upon her face?

Could Yeats return within a Grecian Urn
  to let a hand rub ashes desire?
Could Maya rise and her soul apprise;
  would Mississippi still burn in righteous fire?

How would Neruda fair in the moons cold glare,
  if in despair he was awake?
What would Whitman sing, what quote would Kipling bring,
  if Heaven them both forsake?

I cannot speak for poet meek,
  nor tell the story as if it were true,
Let them rise and the dead surmise,
  what resurrected poets would do

Forever

Karen Bessette

You said you would love me forever,
but that's such a long, long time.
I sat by my window waiting
for you for hours and days.
Soon, winter came trees grew bare.
I closed my eyes and soon
missed the summer of you,
feeling so broken and alone again.

The Tide has Turned

Michael Balner

A pale sun hangs low over the horizon,
and the thickening curtains of heavy blue velvet
move slowly in the warm, moist wind;
the summer is approaching its end.

Your arms—are wide open,
they are soft, welcoming, comforting,
but I'm so tired of the unbearable pressure
imposed onto me
by myself.

A wave after wave, a mellow sadness
files me up to the brim of disintegration.
Yesterday's tide of hope has turned again,
and the exposed sea bottom is covered
by creatures choking in the air.

And so is my hope—
choking in the thickening darkness,
while despair and emptiness
swell out of proportions,
and drag me down, into the pit
of paralysing self-doubt.

No Poet Am I

Gregory Richard Barden

a poet, you say? pardon no, not am I
there's only *one* poet—He writes on the sky
of sunsets and stars, of space without end
with a dazzling bright ink and ethereal pen

of rainbows and sun dogs, anvils and rains
mists from the moors, breeze-tickled plains
of haze-shrouded hills and cloud-crusted peaks
of sunrise horizons with blush on their cheeks

of green flash, auroras, of comets and moons
the fair constellations that rollick and swoon
of bright, stabbing bolts that pierce the dark skies
and spiralling storms with the sun in their eyes

you see …

all that He authors is authentic and true
light years beyond what *my* words can construe
but every-so-often, He blesses this fool
and imparts me the mercy to make me His tool

yes, I'd love to take credit, but I must keep in sight
I'm a pen out of many, with which He may write
so I may seem a bard with these verses I've spun
but regarding *true* poets, there's really … just ...

one.

If You Fall

Graeme Stokes

If you're dropping like the autumn leaves,
  you feel your summer's far behind
When the rain just spills the pain you hold,
  in burst reservoirs of cries
Let me brave that anxious sea you've built,
  we'll swim your tears, you tell me all
I'm the lighthouse that detects your lifeboat,
  and I'll guide you if you fall.

If this cynical world is crushing you,
  through non comprehending eyes
And breaks are running away from you,
  I'll hand the baton, get you home and dry
Let my warm hand be your thawing star,
  my words be your winter shawl
Take a leap of faith, I'm your angel net,
  and I'll cushion you if you fall.

If you're suffering, hurt and grieving,
  for a soul you held so dear
I'll be the heart to lay a wreath in,
  I'll be an Omnipresent ear
I'll be by your side if you need to talk,
  or just say nothing at all
The scars will mend through the stitch of time,
  and I'll soothe you if you fall.

If you need to speak your hopes and dreams,
  my door is open to confide
Pour your worries so they flow downstream,
  empty your cluttered mind
I'll be your legs to jump the hurdles,
  obdurate ladder for the wall
Put in me your trust, when you reach the top,
  and I'll catch you if you fall.

Poema Du'o

Jana Randall Pollard

Two poems diverged where the poet stood,
Meandered down a winding path,
And neither, beginning where they should,
Nor offering up all that they could,
Torn page from page in the aftermath ;

Of loves sweet charms they rambled on,
Towards a certain destiny,
Lamenting of the coming dawn,
As queen was sacrificed for pawn,
A sure and sudden victory;

A tempest or a promenade,
A tidal wave or a sunny day,
The mocking birds must find it odd,
That each are, in their own way, flawed,
But not so much that they will say;

Two poems diverged where the poet works,
And neither being good enough,
Examining her many quirks,
Her word-filled duty, oft, she shirks,
And coats the page with drivelled fluff.

Nothing More Today

Richard Lambton

Nothing more today,
All thoughts broken
Nothing further can be spoken
When simply being is simply too much
When all around is taken as such,
Seemingly not enough
Yet much more than I can bear
Despite how well my deception may appear.

Equinoxed

Jamie Willis

Balance, counterbalance
An autumn day, a segue into
Libra scales of justice
The Sun and Moon each had their say
It was fair but unremarkable
No one had wonder or exclaim
Mild and even, odds erased
That this could be more
Than just the same.
I've seen about enough of this
To last me until solstice
When its longly dark before the dawn..
Where at least there is a fighting chance
For hope in brighter days ahead...
And something more to write about
Than this mathematical yawn.

purposes in poetry

Matt Elmore

bittersweet tributes soothe rapturous rhyme
perfecting purposes too close to home
epitaphs direct where one does not roam
reflecting holiday wishes within time
revealing sorrows to heal between lines
joyous are those that interpret that zone
inherently apparent within poems
deliberately delicate by design

romantically tragic comic delights
emotionally drain strange admissions
select to inflect on the darkest nights
emphatically passionate renditions
of spirit illuminate divine light
to alleviate earthbound conditions

Landlord's Introspection

Joseph Andrew Miller

The building is quaint enough
On a cosmopolitan corner
Façade could use a spruce
But handsome enough
To welcome guests
And please some passersby
Close look to see the trouble though
Scars and cracks multiply
Windows clouding over
Ducts and pipes are looking rough
The building is 36 long stories
Almost 37 and before long, 38
Shorter than many around
Yet already creaks and sways that high
What could easily be mistaken
For an adequate foundation
The early, lower levels strain
Under their innocent naïveté
Used rough by some of the residents
and neglected in their prime
I'm not happy now
With how my building grows
From once exciting, eclectic form
Now stacks of boring, barren floors
Used for what I'd rather I didn't know
Indeed I admit to ceding to disrepair
In hopes that the parts I hate
Would die
With profound disappointment
In how I've let things go
I find I need to wallow in a figment
That demolition lingers nigh

Puzzle

Brian Benton

With my feet upon the ground
And my head no longer in flames now,
I wonder along a path that helps me
Understand the reasons how.

The pieces fell off the table
And the picture before me
Stopped to look like the reality that
It once appeared to be.

I know they fit together
And the picture appeared complete.
But some pieces must have been wrong
For victory I did not gain, left in defeat.

The battle now long ago far gone.
But the war it wages on.
No more bodies to sacrifice to this effort
And I fear no flag remains to guide on.

Alone I will stand and walk along this shore.
For all that were there I pushed away
In that moment of pain where I lost all meaning
And did not care anymore.

The puzzle of my life I now hold close to my heart.
As a shield for the jabs that will come my way.
As I assemble the things that tore me apart.
I contemplate on their relevance and the sum of the disarray.

These pieces now jumbled and scattered about.
Lay out of order and helping me heal.
I found I'm still searching for something I'm without.
Help me to assemble this puzzle for real.

Contemplation

Olivia Knotts

As I stand on the edge of deepest night
Staring at a sky with absent light
The stars, appear like whispers trailing and thin
Surrounded by the endless void they are trapped within

Tell me... What am I but a single breath
A single spark in a second that sinks to death
A single speck of dust, a droplet from a tear
Washed away by a sea so vast and clear

In this fragile, momentous yet fleeting state
I still search for meaning as I contemplate my fate
Does a plan exist? A deities hand?
Or is my life built on shape shifting sand?

Are we the architects of our own time?
Are lives built with reason, rhyme or crime
Can I paint the void with my wishes and dreams
Can anyone tell me what this all means?

Is everything real upon which we gaze?
Does it matter to us, when so brief are the days?
In each step taken we leave our imprint and sound
In each choice we make, do we become unbound?

Existence, barely audible is a quite tune
A distant umberance reflected by a distant moon
For there are no answers, no offer of a key
make if it what you will, we are what we choose to see

Our existence is etched into time and stone
We will still sing our own song then die alone
And though the void will never speak
We and all that come after, will still continue to seek

For we are more than flesh and mealy bone
Humanity, the question that remains unknown
For in every doubt, there is a truth we still scramble to chase
Until we have to admit

The Wager of Life

Hahona Scribe

Beneath scattered skies
burlesque cloud formations jostle
souls bared in unadulterated ardour
colloquial celestial foreplay
& the rain beats upon this tortured flesh
my weather torn body of scorn
precipitating rambunctious rebellion

Manifesting transcendental escape
thunder cracks
roars as the master of a domain
peels to a rhythmic beat
yet my forlorn postulations
be my own

Dream purger
you have no claim to my slumber
& so this scene plays out
manoeuvring thoughts
like chess pieces in my mind
mercury steels these veins
engorging inclement mood
flaccid parchments hang limp

So this is the wager of life
a dollar each way
cedes a tenuous foothold
persevering in vain
serenading elusive victory
feeble flesh subjugates
& the commentator utters
scratched from the rat race
please yield!

Crumbs

Fadi Yousef

At the park
Feeding my thoughts to the birds
Examining the nooks and crannies
Of a day with its wings clipped
My imagination grounded
and unable to soar
To write love letters to the sky
At the mercy of the hours
Growing stale between my fingers
As the sun begins to peck
At the horizon
And shades of pigeons fight
For the afterlife of dusk
My bag growing lighter
As it fills with crumbs of darkness
And moonlight begins to nibble
On the earth's crust
As everything disperses
Towards hungry dreams

Waterborne

Corey Reynolds

water is what I need
I see it pour I watch it cascade
rivers and streams flow to and from
this ocean of my youth and of my dreams
water contains all the drops of my heart
beating away as time evaporates and returns
individual and unique in its misty spray
traveling through poison and darkness
open daylight and clouds of itself
taking turns leaving me and returning
reborn as an ocean blue
to my adoring senses
keeping me alive inside
I remember it well

Before You

Hassan Yusuf Maina

"Before you, life was just a dream
Untold stories seemed like a mere scheme
And after you, they became a true chance to win
A decision to make, a path to begin

Before you, life was just a scale
No love, no joy, no heart to hail
And after you, it became a vector
Guiding me to life's beacon, like a protector

Before you, life was just an image
No aspirations, no decisions to engage
And after you, it became a mirror
Reflecting tomorrow, clearer and clearer
Before you, life was undefined
No title, no cover, no story to find
And after you, it became refined
Famed and recovered, a new life designed"

Enter

Susanne West

Enter the eyes
of the shunned ones
that lead
to the heart
that leads
to the hurt
that leads
to the Infinite
that dissolves
all the names
that made
us two
that remember
us now
as One

Island

Bardin Boyd

just for a minute,
could my relevance
become your responsibility?

i've lost the faculty to
write my own lines.
spending time
constructing culpable
deniability
while waiting for the plot
to thicken.

love is an island.
make me into a peninsula.

Fear of the Dark

Katja Viitamäki

My child
don't fear the dark
You will find your sun
in the rainbow park
Run and play
sing the songs of joy
Catch the stars my boy

In the garden of youth
the birds and butterflies
will dance and celebrate
the days of innocence
Your playground is here
to take you everywhere
So sing the songs of joy
Catch the stars my boy

Cotton Candy Clouds

Rose Marie Streeter

Memories come alive
as sleepy thoughts
tiptoe into view
of gorgeous sunsets
'n cotton candy clouds...

mind gathers up
days gone by
with Angel
serenades
waltzing into
reminiscent places
we once
shared on earth

eyes gaze
into the vast
horizon...
as tiny
white bubbles
float straight
to my heart...
carrying love
notes filled
with promise
of evermore...

sleepy thoughts
finally doze
into land of slumber...
where Paradise dreams
carry me
to rainbows end...
right into your
waiting arms
of Heavenly Bliss....

Losing my Emoji

Terry Bridges

I'm religious to insanity.
Needing the added reassurance
Of everyday familiar things.
How I switch the morning kettle on.
Rington's teabag, 2 Sweetex and milk,
Stirred a definite number of times.
But now there's sink holes in my heart.
I'm losing my emoji.

They've disappeared down the Internet.
Where are my loves and smiley faces?
I want them back again and soon.
It's no fun not being able to compliment
A particular poem or immortal line.
I scroll away, an old favourite appears.
Half-heartedly I celebrate and hope,
But I'm losing my emoji.

Visual characters displayed on-screen.
How trivial, but how much they mean to us.
Cartoon emotions that communicate
Our despair, happiness or care.
And I'll like you if you like me.
Vain as we are we reciprocate
Each seething passion. What I don't like
Is losing my emoji.

Flight

Tom Cleary

Fly me to the moon
with the feathers of your fingers
and wingspan of your eyes
aloft the breeze of your voice.

Empty of Desire

Joseph Gallagher

The sunlight like in some Dickinsonian poem
Slants from Biblical clouds to bruise
This hayfield with its brilliance...
I am neither bee nor beekeeper, but a guest
That watches her gather gold from honeycomb

Smoke to calm the hive that heaves and buzzes
This small universe of guarded trusting bliss—
All the drones the worker bees in motion...
And I am motionless.
And for all this molten smouldering beauty
I am deeply blessed.

Enraptured by the dance she does
To the tune of hum and buzz...
Wings fanning, flickering, a scent of warning .
Her warm brown eyes are so disarming—
I want you more than the stolen honey
Clinging to my fingers...

The golden filaments like a holy ring
About your honeyed hair—
A nimbus of nectar.
That late Autumn afternoon sunlight
Set us both on fire...
And strangely your impossible beauty
Stuns me empty of desire.

Arrivals and Revelations

Linda Adelia Powers

Without provocation, without plans
Before all commitments, absolute discretion
Relief calm and bright, silence
Breathing hope in the world.
What moans in the night longing
Where is the one still sweet and loving
Laughing, living goodwill and delight?
How to find completion in time?
Withdraw interference, take infinite pains
Ask only for endlessly rewarding affinities
Promise support from belief and fond pride.
In the light future of waxing new moons
They have predicted a spiritual clime
When someone has given her heart
Then the mysterious practice of grace
Will not be despised, will be revived and
Oh, what arrivals and revelations
There will be.

Another

Tom Cleary

Always treat your shadow well.
Let it follow you by day
more faithful and accepting
than even the most loyal pet,
attached as a splash of cool shade.
Let it search the library of time
within your dreams,
writing its own silhouetted songs
to an innocent darkness.

Beautiful Dream

Janet Tai

Sweet dream....
Entered my slumber
Sweet dream...
Painted me
A glorious picture;

Sweet dream....
Had me cavorting
Down a busy street
Full of people;

Everyone.....
I came across
Greeted me with
Smiles and hugs;

Everyone...
Knew my name
I felt ecstatic
Like a celebrity;

I was...
Over the moon
Twirling and sashaying...
In excitement
In joy;

Suddenly
A wrong twirl
Had me stumbling
To the ground;

Thud!
I opened my eyes
I found myself
On the floor

Beside the bed;

Dazed...
I was back to
Reality
Oh... Sweet dream
That was some
Ride!

Forest of Dreams

Fouzia Sheikh

Where was I last Friday night?
Within the forest
of dark dreams
Of twists and turns
and nothing honest
Everything is deceiving
The deep trees
Hide chaos unravelling
Seeing the mists rise
Left and right,
Like the leathery fog
that heaves and steams
While the wind,
that tossed in the tattered tree,
And danced alone
with the last mad leaf
Scattered like
dust and leaves,
when the mighty
blasts of October
The beauty of the trees,
the softness of the air,
the fragrance of the grass,
speaks to me.

You Enchant Me

Hahona Scribe

Your very breath
carries my hope
Your vision
holds the scribes
of my footprints
Your heart
beats the pace
my journey
shall be lead

In your eyes
my existence is lost
lakes of ethereal peace
love consummated
'neath passion's tide

Your very touch
spells the degree of fire
Your caress
melt emotions
wanton desire
cascades unabated

Your tears
burn my flesh
Your ache
my very own—
dissolving the grip
of my heart's ease
Your pain shatters
the veil of peace
& so I sacrifice
my resonance
to envelop your being

Like a halo
of Angels' wings

you are
the soft autumn leaves
that caress mother earth
in a bed of tranquility
you are
my breath of hope
my one
and only love

Irish Wristwatch

Steve Wheeler

Come wear an Irish wristwatch. Play
Hot hopscotch in the hotchpotch hay
Tick tock to twine the trickling hours
Tirades in twisted trysting towers
A rawly widened ridden way
All down toward the Galway Bay

Should Sligo sap the slinger's sling
How shall the singer slow her song?
Without its writhing withered wrong
Of such shall Sligo sing along
Tis for the craic we breathe each day
All down along the Sligo way

Through Dublin down to bubbling sea
The drifting Liffey rift flows free
Beneath the Ha'penny Bridge it blows
Past Temple Bar in fulsome throes
The Irish wristwatch plays its hand
Éireann go Brách! This dreaming land!

I Heard The Angels Cry

Valerie Dohren

Across the golden sunset sky
I heard them cry, I heard them cry
I heard the silvered angels cry—
I asked them why, I asked them why!

They looked at me with saddened eyes
Across the skies, across the skies
Across the dark'ning twilight skies—
"What shall we do if love all dies?"

That they should be so deep forlorn
My heart was torn, my heart was torn
My heart was so completely torn—
A sorrow which could not be borne.

They said that they were so afraid
Their hands they laid, their hands they laid
Their hands they then so gently laid
Upon their hearts—where love is made.

They thought, one day, their hearts would die
It made me sigh, it made me sigh
It made me breathe a heartfelt sigh—
So this, to them, was my reply:

I told them not to be downcast
This will not last, this will not last
This will not yet forever last—
That they will know when it has passed.

And furthermore, don't be affright
You'll see the light, you'll see the light
You'll see the light so hold on tight—
For everything will be alright.

That love will never ever cease
So be at peace, so be at peace
So be at long eternal peace—
And from your fear find sweet release.

Sea Poem

Amanda Earthwren Gazidis

Flotsam and jetsam,
shore spume
feet dislodging
small stones crunching,
approaching the
'great white stuff.'

Dreams forged
cobwebs blown away
discarded
diving into a feeling
disintegrating static stanzas
but crashing and frothing
onto the beach.

We cannot contain
our wildness
overspilling,
unpredictable
like these water curls
spilling over shell fragments.

Alive aware awakened
from academic slumber
where heads are buried
deep in the sand.
Celebrating life instead
drinking it in.

No longer floating
and bobbing
on the ebb and flow
but submerged tossed turned
drunk and dazed
by sea, salt and sand.

This is what I've been missing all these years.

Uncle Frank: Black Dog

Sid Oates

Uncle Francis was a mogul
One of Yorkshires richest millionaires
A self-made city grandee
From selling stocks and shares
CEO at Goldman Sachs
That enjoyed the city lights
That rubbed shoulders with Prime Ministers
While dining out at White's

Frank was a city big-wig
That bought his clothes from Saville Row
A Capitalist grand master
With a yacht in Saint Malo
Considered by the 'Old Boy's Clique'
As a Captain of the Game
A cultured Old Harrovian
A bon vivant by any other name

An ex-Lieutenant Colonel
Black Watch Highland Brigade
Charging forth on Juno Beach
As a single piper played
No longer a consociate
Of the city glitterati
Or Chairman of the Kingston Branch
Of the local Tory Party

Now he's sitting in his potting shed
Every hour every day
Drinking dirt-cheap whiskey
To pass the time away
He doesn't read or watch TV
Or seldom speaks at all
As he endures in isolation
Just starring at the wall

His clothes are worn and sullied
His trousers soiled and stained
With dirt behind his fingernails
Irremovably ingrained
Gone the days of manicures
And coiffured slick backed hair
Since being bitten by the 'black dog'
In truth he doesn't really care

His hands are rough and calloused now
And stained with nicotine
That tremble in-between each drink
Where once a sturdy grip had been
The garden once his haven
Now overgrown and wild
Reflects the tangled thoughts within
Of a man once reconciled.

The shed's a silent witness
To the battles fought inside
Where memories and shadows
So fraudulently try to hide
Yet in the stillness of the night
A single tear may fall
For the man who sits in silence
Just staring at the wall

Wondrous Twilight

Rose Marie Streeter

Pastel colored ceiling
embraces,
twilight sky…
imagination leapfrogs,
'if only I could fly'

Veils of light,
soft shadows…
waltz,
before mine eyes…
I wonder 'bout the magic,
keeps me,
hypnotized…

I gaze
in pure amazement…
as moon 'n stars make love…
afterglow, visually awesome…
galaxy,
extends huge hug

I can't…
explain the feeling,
calmness…felt within
could it be, anticipation?
wonders,
to begin…

When twilight
shadows tiptoe…
make pathway
into dreams …
peaceful sounds
of nature…
whisper
me to
sleep

Pretence

Bruce Hart

Be careful what you wish for,
And who you want to be…
We predicate, premeditate
Most things in our destiny

We search for something special,
Yet wallow in the past…
What is our true potential?
It's ourselves we need to ask

We trouble and toil relentless,
Some stumble with each step...
We live our lives eventless
To them vanish, in regret

Tomorrow soon to happen,
Mind and matter takes its course...
Our history, our brutality
And our latest Trojan Horse

Pretence can be a curtain,
We often hide behind…
Pretentiousness too certain
For much of my mankind

Seconds Past Never Last

Richard Lambton

Seconds past never last
Not even the shadows they cast
Despite the cost
Of moments lost,
Forever gone
Yet always going
Somewhere beyond what is shown
And what is knowing.

Nocturne

Betty Santella

A thousand mouths of fire pronounce your name,
Breaking the silence that aborts the night.

Tin stars
on a charcoal sky,
draw your face wherever I go.

The round moon, is nothing more than cotton,
Drinking in the puddles that the rain forgot.

The empty cobblestone street remained,
Waiting for who stole my illusion.

Sonorous prelude
Inspired by your love,
inconstant life has lowered the curtain.

All Because of You

Rufus Daigle

The same love that drives the wind
Takes the turn of the rose
That swings the kiss into
The bloom
The same hope that lights the flame
Takes the stars to stage
That frees the tears beyond the dam
The same wings that lifts the sail
Sold the barley to the field of dream
The same wax that freed the light
Cloaked the dagger that sheared the lines
The same heart that was broken
Was healed by the flower
that left the seed
Behind
All because of you

Blues for Coltrane

Jim Meany

I dream in the essence of blue
Soar into the starry night
I excise the phantasm
Of original sin
Move slowly to a beat
Laid down by the jazz gods
Torn from their sharpened bite
I float on heavy air
That cradles my being
In waves of sound
Music rages through my body
As I slide down
On the wings of angels
And spin between notes blown
In heavenly delight
I morph into space
Float gently by the sun
Lost in the love of all I see
And taste and smell and feel
Can this be real
I am a changeling
A songbird who blows his tune
And howls his madness to the moon
I feast on gentle staccato rhythms
And casually dance
As the willows whine
So go ahead and bow
Before your God
Because I choose mine
Not so much a holy being
As a cosmic note played out
In infinite time

Reverie

Peter Rimmer

Rain on my roof
Is a welcome hug
A blessing.

The ghost of laughter
Echoes down the spent years
Shades of my people
Etched indelibly on this being that is me.

These hollow shells
Whisper of a lost sea
Fleeting moment in time
Memories now.

Sadness rides me from time to time
Taken unawares
A knot of grief constricts my throat
Tears well streaks of sorrow
Wash my face
A weight upon my chest.

Unguarded moments
Sudden visions of tears and laughter
Reverberate through every fiber of my being
Sending me into a reflective reverie.

Overwhelmed with regrets I cannot address
The time for last goodbyes
Saying the things that were left unsaid
Has passed and gone
Forlorn, there's no going back
There is nothing I can say
That will change anything.

Where Anthems Sing

E. C. McCaffrey

Proud haste can pave a way for the rich
When gold has becomes a loathsome dust
And those who gather hungry in its ditch
Only taste the bitter pith of their own lust

Idle minds always blame the silver tongue
With claims a calloused hearts can only take
Accusations seem to hold a smoking gun
Whenever poverty turns into plague

How fat around the middle is the guild
From a wealth made by a nation we call free
Yet on the shores of burden we still build
The ramparts of another's bravery

Stitched by lines of blood and innocence
Corners of a promise between the stars
Anthems with a verse for dissonance
On scrolls that bear proof of every scar

The dotted lines are blurred by years of strain
Ink smeared parchment swearing by a lie
With hands that wear the blood of power's stain
And those who fought against its changing tide

Now the canticle no longer swells
Yet still, its song is heard in empty shells

'Tread Gently,' said the Gentry

Ryan Morgan

What strange adventure lies
In wait over this stile?
The path is carpeted
In grass and quilted
With bursts of clover's
Drifted purple, and to walkover
Those periwinkle petals
Might detrimentally unsettle
The fae creatures whose abodes
Are contained in ditches and hedgerows.
If I tread on these amethysts, I might
Accidentally antagonise some wild sprite.

And then what would happen to me
If I draw the attention of the Sidhe?
Would I be placed in torpor and led around
Dazedly that corner and then be bound
To abide amongst the Blessed Folk
As time's pendulum suspends its stroke?
Thus imprisoned by the Unseely Court
I'd at once wizen when freed of their sport.
When placed back at this stile,
I'd flake and crack to a dust-pile
And die centuries hence
For my summary offence.

Vagabonds

Gregory Richard Barden

alkaline streets
bleed with the dreams of
humanity, angels in
bootlegged Blahniks

flutter wings of
dubious intention
a silent wisdom of the gods
spills empty pockets ...

gilded pillars of
Olympus, brought to
ruin by pushcart
pariahs—

the tattered pages
life scribbles on—
a cursive profanity to rub
each nescient nose

sawbucks for
flesh by the warm
handful—strains of
the night, bound

sewer vents
puff their vile breath
as vagrants bask in
putrid warmth ...

every horrid
tale plays out
in actuality
and yet, above ...

the precious,
resplendent heavens
witness ...
all.

Once Again

Archie Papa

The war against poverty will be fought with ink
those in the war room are not who you think
strategically sound and invisibly planned
the writers and poets have taken a stand

Here we deliver each powerful word
around the world the echoes are heard
crafted and honed with the greatest of care
the peace in our souls we willingly share

Those in need cannot rest assured
the ills of greed can ever be cured
with these words from our mighty pen
to bring health and happiness once again

Moss

Martin Attard

I sit here and ponder the moss on the floor
Everything else has been pondered before
By pondering I'm really just wasting time
Squandering moments both yours and mine.

I uselessly wonder if the moss ponders me
Sat still and verdant, outwardly serenely
It's concept of purpose must be alien
As its life passes by, then begins again.

How did it get here, was it kicked from a roof?
Did a disgruntled lyricist use it as proof
That beauty and meaning don't require truth
And that gathering moss is the ruin of youth.

Canvas Blues

Kate Cameron

Mocking me in their pallid stacks
inviting or beguiling me onto the rack
tormenting rhythmic interludes
how do I capture enraptured
esoteric passions
in my mind,
towering twisting angels
cloudbanks holding gilded light
sublime visions

silken petals & ermine moths
champagne skies
lilies glow
soft as snow
starry nights
candle light
soft baby cheeks
canvas blues
hope on fire
not to miss
its soft hued kiss

Word Moths

Graham Rhodes

Another one
of those nights
where the words
dance at the
end of the room
too vague to be
caught and assembled
into logical sentences,
scattering like moths
when the light goes out

They

Tim Queen

shuffle the street
a race of shabby saints

exploding into a thousand
pigeons conquering the

invasion of evening
estranged between

darkened buildings
blessed by moonlight

obscured by morning
disappearing under

solemn bridges
dreams arrive…

on the 1st of the month.

Have a Glimpse

Peter Rivers

Within me
See miracles,
Dances, and songs to be sung
Each day's long end
Totally surrounded
All silence and noise
Our constant
Contradiction
Then blink…

Disposing of a Mattress

Ryan Morgan

A wobbly, unstable
Strain of springs
And stale sweat.
How can something so horizontally hard
Be a blancmange when vertical?
I drag my former cradle of rest
Into an upright position.
It's a menhir of unmanageability,
And it eyes me mockingly
With its faded tufting.

I spread my arms
And step into its embrace
Face pressed into the dustiness,
The decades of old skin cells.
I breathe in the remnants of younger me,
Infusing myself with youth's discarded vigour.
But the mattress has the advantage
And we dance the bear hug waltz
Shambling around the floor
As if it's the night's last call.
My grip slips from the seams
And the mattress collapses in laughter.

I jump on it like in the good old days
And fold it like a taco,
Squeezing it shut
In tandem with my molars.
I mount the scissored springs
And hog tie it by the handles,
Grunting with the grind.
I slip off its back and collapse
In an ecstasy of exhaustion
Then grab it by the fringes
To manhandle it down the stairs.

Compress it into the car boot
Like a comedy mafia hood,
And then off to the dump.
The mattress is now exhausted
Quiet save for the odd strain and shift,
But all the fight has gone out of it.

It's not even 9 am.
I want to go back to bed.

Symphony of the Senses

Emmanuel Chimezie

Can you see the eyes singing—
Songs solemn, like the peacock in the morning?
Can you see the eyes singing?
Books piercing, snarling, in the template of
the heart, crocking?

Can you hear the trees humming—
Doves cooling, like the pastoral angel cooing?
Can you hear the trees humming?
Words healing, weaving—
the weevils barking and howling?

Can you feel the breeze coming—
Whitish latex, pure, like the Eden eternal,
in the cortex soothing?
Can you feel the breeze coming—
Silent scream, soliciting
in the field of souls, souling?

I Saw My Father's Ghost

Brandon Adam Haven

I saw my father's ghost,
As daisies wither to die.
His form, rotten and amort,
Silenced in his lurid glow.

I saw my father's ghost,
Bellowing the crisp air,
Bleeding into a new form
Where he wished to remain.

I saw my father's ghost,
As his ashes I spread,
Staring firm into me
As they succumb to the wind.

I saw my father's ghost
In memories long forgotten,
Where we hugged tight;
Violence was not an option.

I saw my father's ghost;
My soft heart melted.
I start wailing in agony,
Void of an empty embrace.

I saw my father's ghost
Where no solace is left.
Even with all these tears,
Each one falls bereft.

I saw my father's ghost,
Staring through the brush
Of a thousand chimes,
None of which were mine.

I saw my father's ghost;
The cold realization hits
As weeping leaves blow,
Reminding me I'm left all alone.

Rhyme

Bruce Hart

The sky begins to darken,
Another false goodbye…
Love at the helm, in its own realm
Another chance to crucify

There's always one expression,
That doesn't sound so true…
There's always one dimension
That doesn't add up to you

I love you more than ever,
After what you said today…
But then I thought, whatever?
It's tomorrow's yesterday

Give into me in infamy,
And tell me that it's you…
Let me unwind, in one more rhyme
And wish, that it were true

A Rainy Night

Graham Rhodes

Outside
the rain falls.
Bouncing across the tarmac.
Blurring the yellow lines.
A man
turns up his collar,
and walks faster.
Bad weather for the street cats,
that stops their prowling,
hiding under shelter,
under sheds behind walls.
Tonight even the rats
will stay home.

To Love

Emmanuel Chimezie

I told love to be soft, but she shouts aloft—
I told love "Let's build a cubicle,"
—she hums
to my ears in words mystical.
I asked for silence;
she sang in riddles.
I pleaded for mercy—
she conceded a prank... I kissed her
patterns—she cries, still, without aim.

She cuddled me with her cold hands; I sleep
on her loan—A debtor to her music, a parallelism
to her sighs! A beggar to her phases—she smiles
in labyrinthine ways. I told love to be soft,
but she shouts aloft!

Halfway Hill

Steve Wheeler

Bury me under the Halfway Hill
Where the swallows fly
and the earth is still
And the tall clouds float
'cross the meadows green
Like a timeless dream

Bury me under the Sycamore tree
Where the ancient bones
of the warriors weep
And the distant echoes
of the children ring
From the songs they sing

Thankful

Michael Balner

All my deeds, like pearls on a thread,
Some were good, and some were—less;
I'm thankful for each one of them,
They've led me to this very place.

The river of time, the steady flow,
From a beginning to the very end,
I'm thankful for each tiny moment
Of being here and now, awake.

Sometimes myself, and sometimes not,
Sometimes I'm found, but often—lost;
I'm thankful for the darkest night
In which I found what matters most.

Rising up from my bleeding knees,
My body bruised, still, here I stand;
I'm thankful for the wounds and pain
Which made me the man I am today.

fast words

neil mason

fast words
tumbling from my mind
fast words run across an empty page
filling up quicker than a bank holiday beach
not even room for a small comma
fast words race to piece a story together
everyday objects brought to life
fast words of a microwave poet
are ready to read in a few seconds

An Autumn Song of Verlaine

Robert Atkins

The sighing strings
Of violins,
Autumn drone;
A wound at heart
As languor starts,
Monotone.

No oxygen,
A faintness, then
A clock chime;
With tears that fall
Remember all
The lost time.

I take my flight
In breeze's spite
Fly in grief;
An errant soul,
No aim no goal,
A dead leaf.

The Graveyard of Empires

Brandon Adam Haven

Memoirs buried beneath withered stone,
Burnt to decay the hardened walls of home.
Countries of dreams, feverishly plighted,
Now destitute, the remorse of love divided.
We sink together to aphonic pits unknown,
Crumbling without repair, this broken home.
Together we once thrived; now apart we die.
We've become the graveyard of empires.
Ask yourself why…

Winter Approaches

Emile Pinet

winter approaches
snowflakes tumble from the sky
a sprinkle of white

As brisk breezes scatter leaves around,
Autumn colors confetti the ground.

Winter winds howl through barren branches
shaking off any remaining leaves.

Mother Nature is in transition;
striping the scenery yet again.
The naked trees are in remission
till Spring showers, water them with rain;
and green canopies supplant the plain.

Deep Purple Shades of Melancholy

Lorna McLaren

The dark arrived so suddenly,
unlit, not even by the moon,
in deep purple shades of melancholy
when even the stars forgot to bloom.
All around the silence reigned,
a pregnant pause in time,
as if the world had stopped momentarily
while waiting to re-align.
Out of this wilderness of apathy
it jolted once again to life
as the moon crept from the shadows
to slice the darkness like a knife.
Stars began emerging,
with all the light they could accord,
to gift us with normality
as night was once again restored.

this melancholic mood

Steve Howkins

this melancholic mood I'm in
it longs to let the sunshine in
so that autumn feels like spring
when the birds begin to sing
this melancholic mood

this melancholic mood I feel
it longs to see the sky reveal
its sunshine face behind the clouds
with sunbeams through the misty shrouds
this melancholic mood

this melancholic mood of mine
it always comes at autumn time
when the leaves lie all around
and the earth is winter bound
this melancholic mood

this melancholic mood's black dog
it lingers like the morning fog
when the days grow dark and dim
and we long for joys of spring
this melancholic mood

this melancholic mood won't go
the alcoholic afterglow
it leaves me feeling kind of numb
just longing for a glimpse of sun
this melancholic mood

this melancholic mood I'm in
it longs to let the sunshine in
so that autumn feels like spring
when the birds begin to sing
this melancholic mood

How Small I Am

Richard Harvey

See the river flow as time floats by
And as the wind blows time sure can fly
I see the mountains how tall they stand
I look at me, how small I am

I see the sunshine it gives me light
The stars I ponder, awestruck each night
I search for meaning, there is a plan
I look at me, how small I am

I see your beauty as you're standing there
So many people, for all of you I care
I see your heartbeat, I see your hands
I look at me, how small I am

Of all the beauty and wonder seen
You are the best of all that's been
You are majestic, you are so grand
I look at me, how small I am

short story

Leslie C. Bertrand

Once we were lovers,
Then we were friends;
Now we are strangers,
And the love story ends.

Spectre

Terry Bridges

An ennui of exhaustion
Dead numb November mist
No cry of bird on the wing
Penetrates the washed leaden sky
No wind to whisper a note

The silent universe rotates
Gyre or gyroscope
Dark matters tumble in the mind

Under an alien sun
Eldritch beings contemplate God
Or whatever exists
Laugh at folly like kids

I saw a ghost once
Floating in air like gossamer

Cliché

Mieczyslaw Kasprzyk

There is a wind blowing
And the cobbles are glistening,
Wet after the shower.
I am walking, unwrapping
The cellophane off
the cigarette packet
(The craving was
too much for me again).
The wind blows my coat open
As I walk leaning against it,
Pulling out a fag,
Like some Harry Lime
Going to an appointment.
I am a cliché.

The Man for this Time

Kenneth Wheeler

The man of this age,
Is the man for this time
The man for this moment
Is the man you will find.
He's there in the shadows
Awaiting your call to arrive
When feeling at your lowest
Struggling hard to survive
Don't leave it for too long
Call upon His precious name,
In anxiety or even in a song,
Or moments of deepest pain
Call upon the One who will
Heal and drive away your pain
Give hope with new life to gain.
In the time that still remains
Lord Jesus is His holy name.

Wings 'n Things

Rose Marie Streeter

Butterflies, dragonflies
siblings on a quest
gossamer wings, favorite things
captured in a net

Fireflies, twinkling eyes
lightening in a jar
belly laughs, twinkling glass
fantasy all ours

Butterflies, dragonflies
nature once explored
fireflies, twinkling eyes
memories evermore

My Little Box

Richard Harvey

Here I sit in my little box,
as the world revolves outside
Windows closed and the door is locked
And you know I'm petrified
Tick tock the sound of the clock
and my beating heart collide
Back and forth I rock and rock
In the darkness, my eyes opened wide
The voice inside my head just mocks
And it seems that it never subsides
All I hear is talk, talk, talk
And fills my head with lies
If I only had the key to this lock
Then out of here I'd fly
But here I sit in my little box,
as the world revolves outside

November Moon

Fouzia Sheikh

I have been watching
the crows and now it is dark
Together they led night
into the creaking oaks
Under them I hear
the dry leaves walking.
That blind man
Gathering their feathers
before winter
In the November's moonlight
By the dim road
that the wind will take
The chill of the cold night
Rustling with the wind
In the pale moon's
Half-light.

Simple Dreams

Peter Rimmer

Today dissolves in sunshine
A gentle breeze blows down the avenue
Ruffling street trees
Puffs of cloud softening sky
Drifting by.

Spring shines warmth
Painted brightly on my face
Sitting in my accustomed space
Back against the wall
Inhaling the fragrance of the afternoon
Cool beer in hand
I could want for little more.

Simple things
Make the best dreams
Today a radiant smile
Trails off a ways till
Evenings cool grace
Still some hours away.

Parked here I am happy
Eyes grow heavy weary
Maybe soon I'll drift a bit
Birdsong serenading
The lengthening day
Simple dreams
Are fine by me.

A Healthier Today

Peter Rivers

Household hazards
Curly, unruly, fast-growing
demand
Dangerous pregnancies
Making crisis
Doctors diagnose
medical mysteries
Critical condition
3.3 billion
Workforce cuts
Toxic foods
Transmitted infections
Pounds of butter
Cases fall in US
Return to work
Flash and burn
Chronic health issues

psychiatric shampoo voodoo

(moisturize my lifeless volume)

Matt Elmore

seeking clarity I only wish to be flake free
invigorate completely your formula recovery
blinded reminded cleanse me intelligently
infused with honey bunny so soft and shiny
innovate my style for black orchid mint quality
massage thoroughly for total damage therapy
throughout my dry animal derived volatility
perpetually dirty forever wash rinse and repeat
moisturize my lifeless volume with durability
such lush lather matters for this fresh full body
with your cucumber water snake oil technology
demand our prime strands stand in harmony
optimize our lives together by conditioning me

Random Tadpoles

Lorna McLaren

A mass of squirming black tadpoles/ hundreds and hundreds of them/ soon after their return to India/ were photographed visiting a local/ systems of hoses from the burn. Seven years later, now with three/ ourselves with Uncle Matt doing/ passes without incident on/ we have nothing to report other than/ that's jist never going tae happen. That was the point at which it was/ I had a bit of campaigning for/ a spare 12 volt water pump. Talking of the burn I think we/ may have acquired ourselves a/ couple of wild ducks. Anyways, as usual, we finish up/ by mundane litter picking/ but we all ken that she/ not her former boss, would be/ wishing that the next four weeks/ with all your mistakes in full view/ you learn on the job in the fishbowl. I was trying to ignore the consequences/ and not just asking the questions. I'm ready for the next task/ rather than being thrown in at/ the deep end with no running water/ so we'll continue our isolation/ and you know what you need to do.

For Who Am I to Speak and Answer Whys

Karin J. Hobson

So I would ask myself the same question?
This is a very small book in the Old Testament
the 'whys' is that they genuinely want to know
This is he/she
Because everyone phrases it that way
answering this question is a lifelong quest
thinking about the categories that we are in,
Furthermore, identity is the all-encompassing,
it has to do with human existence
It's a very simple question.
Until you try to answer it.

Healing Touch

Donna Smith

And the sun dons the clouds like a crown
Motionless spirals of dreamless sleep
By tempest or delicate rain
She drew the wind
A wail, a cry, a howl unmatched
Still the hope and still the dreams
The world within me
Fore waking to renewal
As healing touch holds solace high
Slips long the burnished banister
And the glowing haze of fog
A flame of fiery ferocity
Of unjustifiable feasts of death
Silhouette by the moon, a silver lining ghost
Tumble down paths forgotten
Sprouted from ignorance
Buried neath fodder for millennia
I keep dancing all alone
Like gentle Autumn rain
For my soul with yours elopes.

Delirium

Jessica Ferreira Coury Magalhães

In the rain, I caught a fever
I was not quite here nor there
In the dark I thought I kissed you
But I was blowing kisses in the air

No one knows the many visions
I have behind this blank, dire stare
Although from me you remain hidden
I still see you everywhere.

I don't know how nor when
I will wake up from this nightmare
Will I see your face again
Or will I remain in despair?

Then I recognise you in the distance
Waving your hand to me
I run for the sake of my existence
And at last, reunite with thee.

Dream-Dust Ink

Archie Papa

Here you see them, take a look
found on pages in a book
here they come, there they go
where they stop we'll never know

Rhythm feels and understands
a happenstance of random plans
a game that's only just begun
syllables playing, words are fun

Over one side, down the next
attracting likeness in the text
plucked and polished from thin air
dream-dust ink, I do declare

Time will never take away
words ideas arrange to say
dancing words in every book
here you see them, take a look

The Rose Upon My Grave

Jamie Willis

Could you love me in my darkness
In the shadows of the convex curve
Nestled deep against the womb wall
That often feels more death than birth

Could your fingers touch my petal skin
And risk the thorns beneath the silk
My body has endured much grief
And my heart is bloodied further still

Could your mouth inhale my kisses
And sustain the sting of salted tears
I know the saline chase of sorrow
Stains your dream of holding me right here

Could you stand to watch the prison break
Of sobs that wrack and row away
With hopes once locked within my ribcage
And see the light in me just... fade

Could you love me then?

Could you love me when I've disappeared
Lost in the chloroform of pain
And numb to what made me alive
Could you love whatever trace remained?

Could you love me when I'm telling you,
I'll never be the same?
Because, I'll never be the same.
Could you love the girl that I become...
The rose upon my grave.

Vampires and Verse

Emmanuel Chimezie

I am the vampire, perched on my
sister's diester in siesta—
She daunts my mollusca—I flee above,
Singing like a flea to my distant biomes.
She slaps my face, sparking a vase of venomous verse;
I laugh awake, forlorn, like a folklore shaking.

We dance like farce, felicitating
fallacious, flattered lies,
Meowing and crouching on the couch of our bed of roses—
Inking bread of mosses.
We are murdered, like my mother shattered,
Into yards of unwanted pregnancies.

My father moos his mouth, shouting to ghostly wailings—
With protruding dialysis, stinking and soothing.
I am the vampire, a satire of sackcloth snoring?

dance of amaranth romance

Matt Elmore

velvet purple scarves whirl winds
focusing in fantasy smiling at me
as days chase nights into infinite crush
immortal perfection colors red lip blush
pursed for valuables dripping wet words
heard in luscious supple daydreams
flowering aura of beauty defy my existence
sound sensual imagery refined beyond fine
goddess of bloom in euphonious epiphany
envelope reality of an absolute consent
when positive vibrations smooth moves
energies enact this voracious endeavor
stealing mine eyes before my heart
that I might watch you dance forever

Si Vix Pacem, Para Bellum

Dale Parsons

If you want peace...
The ocean is the body,
a militarised composition
and structure...oceanic trenches.
Field tactics and conduct.
Not a well-defined measure.
Strategic deceptions
influence climate and weather.
Unity and moral,
from the surface to the ocean floor.
The temperature in false equilibrium.
Weapons used, which light intensifies,
damaging the targets...
deep into the photic zone.
Unsheathe the sword
to swim in the ocean.
Wet violence.
Prepare for war.

Insomnia

(Double Acrostic)

Archie Papa

In the mind awake, we see litter and graffiti
never ending plan of what should happen
seconds gather under broken street lights
on their way to somewhere long ago
moments always gaining momentum
new to old from somewhere in between
in the mind asleep, we see glitter and confetti
aligning destiny, fate, and karma

Embedded Gold

Kate Cameron

The Apothecary's rose came to perfection
nestling amongst Bronze Fennel
blue chicory soothed the eyes
in the villa garden

turning to an adjacent page
intense fragrance abandoned to the winds

Antigua long ago
High grade silver—he soldered a frame
Icon of the virgin, a veiled head
engraved

hunting a model in the marketplace
turn of a long neck , an almond eye
he searched the crowd feverishly

the artist left only with embedded gold
cool tiles under sore knees
devotion

stripped of some bitter bark
aromatic herbs strewn sweetly
& when she half smiled
the fates turned

intrinsic weight less
than face value of a moment

in spite of plumes, silks,
pounding heartbeats trembling limbs
a reverie
a reverie

Mustard Butter Horizon

Donna Smith

Sketch me a night sky in a fusion of yellow,
Paint a canvas of sweet marigold.
Cast in a mustard butter horizon,
Honey blended for a sight to behold.

Merge in a tangerine Crayola,
Let the colours all morph and coalesce.
On a canvas of white marble wonder,
As it shimmers a bright opalesce.

Cement it in Citrine and ochre,
Stain it a sunbeam desire.
Dye it a lemonade chartreuse,
Light it in a bright amber fire.

Make it exactly to my liking,
Pattern the blueprint, the design.
Style it to my specification,
Let this one night be all mine.

Each Reach

Stephen Boydstun

Each reach, root, clasp, or grasp,
all flights, all calls, all nests,
all pulsing blood, all valves,
all meters and accounts,
bows of gifts, ties of love,
treasures of loveliness
in being and thinking,
in rainbows and forest,
in commerce and the peace—

Each problem and harvest,
lay and planting for each
breath and cry and suckle,
struggle, rest, and struggle
to grasp and say and make—
are only of life, life
gyring round, rambling to
life wide-waked to wide world
and to itself with you.

Three Poems Knocking on My Door

Rafik Romdhani

I have ignored poetry for three days.
I was busy, observing the world
through someone else's lenses.
The poems I should have written
came knocking on my door,
shouting out my name,
like three girls drunk on palm wine.
The first one had the smell of cinder.
She must have been dancing
and twirling in anger.
The second one was holding
her forehead in her left hand
and stretching her right one to mine
so that I can smell the fresh manicure.
But surprisingly enough, the third one
burst like a tyre into my face
and as I fell completely unconscious,
all the three run jealousy
to the nearest petrol station
to bring gasoline and burn up
the novel that is clouding my mind.

Breaking the Speed Limit

Fadi Yousef

She lives a fast life
Breaking the speed limit
To relationships
Sitting atop her throne
On the back seat of a bike
With a front row seat to danger
Hanging from the edge
Of another bottle of whiskey
Fuel to burn
Yet another romance
Her lips at the root
Of a dying cigarette
As she puts out a kiss
In the ashtray

A black leather jacket
Hanging from the bedpost
Like a rebel flag
To everything unholy
The only thing she needs
To hold her
On another stop
In the wind's highway
As she zips up the night
And grabs her helmet
Runs into the arms
Of the handlebars
Throttling the rising dawn

Hunter's Snare

Ryan Morgan

The white hart ran
With the rising sun

Into the forest
Dark and deep
Slumbering still
On the borders of night.

I followed keen
On instinct's edge,
Unable to rein
The hunter within
From taking the head.

In passion, I pursued
The silver flame,
Dancing and darting
In the darkening deep.
Its fascinating flicker
Just out of reach.

Past the broadleaves,
Curling ferns and soft mosses,
Into hidden root
Of the primeval wood,
Where silent pines
And unsounded snow
Are the only witnesses
To the soul's bones
And the impulses of man.

There,
In the essence of night
Where earth and sky
Are split stark

Black and white,
Breath's fog misted
My snaring gaze.

The white hart vanished
As if it never was at all.
I am left, lost and alone.
And the ignored snow
Has smothered my tracks.

Lulling Lovers

Karin J. Hobson

Silence hums the twilight air save lone hoots
from an owl here and there;
Where unseen masses of emerald green grasses
like tender-white feathers endlessly measure in dreams;
A haunting serenade is suddenly evoked
'neath brilliantly spaced-out diamond
provokes of eternal heavenly bliss

Inquisitive eyes are hypnotized
when 'tween branches bare, become aware
of a most unusual sight;
Tis not sweet scent of lilac,
but pretty placed shades of lavender-laced hues;
A mist so delicately veiling Luna in portrait
like a bride's first day of wed;
What a venerated Moon!
To trance-fix an ogler,
produce a mystical mind-boggler,
speechless and beyond reproach
but, that of Luna lulling lovers
in this magickal nite!

Blue Hour

Gary Richmond

Your words cut me deep to the jugular
Strung together
Like baroque pearls of hate
Illustrating the depth
Of your imaginary angst
A confusion of blame
In your place

You were the one who said "trust me"
And you were the one who said "wait"
You were the one who said "breathe and relax"
So I did, and you spit in my face

Dropping you off
At your Mother's house
After you said that your love
Had gone sour
Sitting by myself
And crying in the dark
All alone
In this silent
Blue Hour

What stops a heart from beating?
When does a love
Lose its power
Wishing for peace
Isn't cheating
Picking sides in this lonely
Blue Hour

I'll scream your name
From the hollows
I'll scream "I love you"
From a cell-phone tower
I'll scream "why me?"
From the depths of my pain
On my own
In this brutal
Blue Hour.

Jimmy's Flare

Imelda Zapata Garcia

It's not just,
that his five o clock shadow
looms as a daunting tower
o'er some
His piercing eyes disarm
with but a tender look
Disrobe shrouded thoughts
to a hum
Gentle touch caresses
hearts that shook
Voice confuses sounds
of where he's from
And he perplexed
questions what's become
This spec of grit
within my written book
Piece of puzzle
of my loin's full sum
I plant a loving kiss
upon his brow
Coax him own
a heavy crown
Point to the matrix
that's bequeathed a vow
Remind him, he is born
of hearth's abound
Place on broad shoulders
prides endow
Within the telling
of his here and now
That we bring fire
upon a dim lit town
As we disperse the truth
of what we've found
He is a son
of heritage which holds
A treasure trove

brighter than gold
A dream once woven
which emboldens
A people's force
awaiting to unfold
Child of setting Sun
a Moon's own glow
Carries most profound
a truth he holds
Promise of a future
bubble he must blow
To burst a raging lie
that has been told

A Blank Canvas

John Castillo

A blank canvas
A reality of thought
Imagination poured
Onto ideas
Colored by intent
Brushed with magic
Magic of vistas
Created by one
Shared with any
Who would open
Their eyes
To possibilities
Accept shifts
In the staid
To include
New ideals
A blank canvas
A place to begin

Winter is Here

Graeme Stokes

It announces itself unceremoniously
in a gruff voice of frosty tones
Its harsh breath, somewhat unharmoniously,
sucks the lifeforce from Autumn's bones
Like a decadent thief in the dead of night,
an unbid thought invading your sleep
An erstwhile threat that's sprung to life
with a brooding vendetta to keep!
Like the cold grin of a creepy stranger,
generating a mounting unease
With the cool precision of a surgeon's scalpel,
it bitterly strips the trees off leaves!
The inexorability of a Roman cohort,
a calculating march of duty
But beneath its exterior of shivering faults
the ice queen projects an ethereal beauty!
A sun's pristine smile, on mornings crisp,
a disguising beard covers the grass
The cocksure Robin's pose, captured on a twig,
a parental hug from heated cars
The chance to dance with gyrating flames,
the mesmeric sway of candles
To relive the first time, with wide eyes again,
pretty snowflakes precipitate angels
The lullabies that play in sound repose
where dreams are cosily housed
Scarves and mittens, rosy cheeks and nose,
winter sustenance to devour!
The stoic creatures that flout hibernation,
majestic reindeer in the park
The gratifyingly warm sensation,
of hot mulled wine poured after dark!
The freezing topic sits divisive
like needle icicles upon a fence
Snugly loved or coldly derided
just like the season's big event.

alone

Stephen James Smith

mute as settled snow
echoing loneliness
travels along the cliff edges
of my muddled mind
a constant companion
in this jumbled heap of mountains
I lock eyes with a god
who turns away
I stumble, I fall
into an abyss of white hell
where winter's setting sun
slants on a knife edge
slicing my fading shadow.
When I realise we are all alone
a sudden spark of fire
rises like flames from a phoenix
its light fire shatters the dark cold
as my loneliness empties
with thoughts of being
alone with you

Beneath the Weight of Becoming

Emmanuel Chimezie

Sharp snip, snippers, my shriek—
yelling,
unique boutique of warbles!
Voices velveting the serenity—
of jagged jungle drums, gritting
my gross grape of spongy sight,
of perfumes—
Lush, mellow billows the Sea
of salty, sour, soaring boar
of rapid, roaring ruminescence,
waking!

Ruminating the truncating shackles—
the litters whispering "Your vein
bleeds, brown cries!"
I am the testament of wagging heads, running—
I am the firmament of withered
leaves, shouting.

Tragic Novel

Fadi Yousef

I go through the rabbit hole
Of imagination
Follow the white light
Of the paper
As an idea pokes through the mind
Rides the brainwaves of synapses
To the inlets of my fingers
Jumping off the boardwalk
Of my pen
Into a sea of other words
All trying to find breath
And survive the currents
Of the rough draft
As letters stretch their limbs
And hold hands in cursive
Figuring to work together
To reach the shore
For a period of rest
But the daylight begins
To crumple at the edges
Waters of inspiration
Hit a dam of writer's block
As the words drown
In a whirlpool in the wastebasket
A romance novel
With a tragic ending

Things that are no more

Kate Cameron

Out into the rippling streaming wheat
the brown hart dancing fled
as fleet as the wind
that strokes my hair and moved the leaves
heavy hoof beats pound the earth
I stilling held her glorious sight

a reverie in gilt sunlight
she ran in leaps down to the farms low fields
where cows drowsed peacefully in August sun
butterflies fluttering on shy white flowers
in little whirls

and once I saw you dance along this street
your hair a fiery mass of curls
a giggle and gaggle of little girls
on light feet, fleet

now across the fields the air is cold
quartz white as ice, the wheat is sheered
and dying then—it saw the white hart leap
as a goddess—mute as stars,
magical and remote as natural laws

as mute as I, the rain is tears
as red leaves fall
as red leaves fall

Write

Natasha Browne

Write me within a dream,
Write me in a stream,
Write my existence,
Write something of resistance.

Write me a story,
Write me an inventory,
Write me on the trees,
Wite me upon the breeze.

Write me in your laughter,
Write me a happily ever after,
Write me in your tears,
Write me in your fears.

Write me across the sea,
Because I am poetry.

Rebel Hearts

Donny Hatch

Obedience etched in the heart of the rebel
Temptation a war in the mind
Both goodness and evil engaged in a battle
By consequence choice is defined

While gratification is temporary
If the master of darkness prevails
The kingdom of light offers infinite life
For the power of love never fails

Forgiveness and mercy are gifts freely given
To anyone searching for grace
But sorrow and misery haunt you forever
if shadows are what you embrace

The Broken Heart

Mark Fuge

I cried to the heavens from a place of desperation,
and God sat quietly at my side.

His mighty hand gently gathered up
the broken pieces of my heart.
Thunder became his needle and lightning his thread.

He drew together strands of grace
as brokenness, fear and rejection embraced.

They entwined in a dance with glory until…
peace enthroned my face.
That peace-stranger, I once knew,
retuned—and I stood healed.

The master surgeon's work
was too great to understand,
describe it I cannot,
deny it, I cannot
and these words come
nowhere near to praise His sweetness
or describe the encounter.

As He arose, God turned and said:
"I came to heal the broken-hearted
and will heal every heart that calls.

No tragedy can best me,
no disaster can prevent me,
no pain will stop the love-flow,
purchased by Jesus on the cross."

Atoms

David Simpson

The atoms in you,
Were made in a star,
Billions of years ago,
So think about,
How old you are,
And be glad that it doesn't show.

seduction of the wolf moon

Matt Elmore

I draw you in with a wet vampire's gaze
hypnotic metabolic magnetic in pull
I lull within you deep animal howls
lips held high to coo vast purple skies
projecting raw volume back up to me
occasionally hiding beyond thin wisps
gasping ghostly ghastly carnal bliss
arousing red dens of carousing denizens
ravenous naked night of sipping shadow
my wolf beam intoxicates foggy memory
romantic pedantic semantically sensual
come to me, run with me, howl for me
circle weak sleeker prey; become my aura
when many do not even notice me
until the next moment they look up
only to feel your most real lightening bite
sinking deep meshed into tender flesh
as I long to watch you stare into my eye
luring love away from the predictable sun
reflecting only a select cosmic suggestion
for you to love my touch upon your face
warm tingle wild throughout your body
I quench hunger deep within your core
feeding animals born bare within your soul

In the Likeness of Stardust

Archie Papa

The toll we pay for the burdens of time
will bear the weight of its wasting
the soul forgiving in the name of love
will share it to the heart's content
From stardust we came, all one and the same
it's our energy you see, moves differently
As heartbeats keep pace, the mind finds a place
for clemency in the trials of reality
Undermine the structure whose barriers ensue
tear down the walls between me and you
in the gravity of truth our fears come undone
in the likeness of stardust, we are one

Flames of Vengeance

Dale Parsons

Go back to the shadow
I am the servant of the secret fire,
and the father of a murdered son
Ethereal voices in orchestral choir,
the singing of a mournful song
A husband to a murdered wife,
flames rise with furies emergence
Some that die deserve life, know,
I will have my vengeance
The dark fire will not avail you,
chorus rising as flames combust
And I am coming with you,
we mortals are but shadow and dust
People want to know how the story ends,
know, you shall not pass
Did vengeance ever make amends,

running fingers through heaven's grass
Go back to the shadow

The Black Moon

Georgia Florence

The black moon
Covets the ocean
A lapping wave
Breaths the last
Grains of love sift closer
To your compass smile
QAs
Broken vessels pull
And tinker

She lights smoked skies
Patiently listens
To bruised hearts
Whiskey laments
Torn wishes on sepia
Smudged Kohl streaks
In Lost diaries
An anchor's regret
In the deep

The night snuffs
Her echo with no return
She is wicked darkness
Comfort and envy
Exhausted sailors
And sirens alike
lay in shadowed places

Their intent to never
Dream again
Lucidity mocks

Tobacco and leather
Embraces
Momentarily reaching
Out beyond
The Harpies giggle
Of their aporetic woes
A fevers sweat beads
The skin
To set the bones

Winter's imps
Light fires
To warm
Grieving feet
Beat out the
Rhythm
Flickered faces
Manically mirror
Each other
Laughter and age lines
Etched deeper
As if they know
They're a tribute

Ragged wretches
Bang the drums
Vulnerable ribs vibrate
Massaging aching hearts
Clashing flagons
Miss not a beat
And dance
For those lost
Too soon
under
The black moon

Saffron Sky

Jamie Willis

The sky was strangely saffron
Like the painter somehow dipped his brush
from amber into crimson's pot
Then worked the canvas in a rush
Right over blue forget-me-nots
To drench what was pastoral
With the fire of a thousand flames
Each burning off the daylight,
None hotter than the searing pain
That rushes through my wounded heart
More Celsius than a lava pour
More Fahrenheit than mercury marks
More Shadrach than a furnace door
The only fourth man standing
Is the one my desperate eye can see
With my peaking desperation...
A Grimm cloaked man's solemnity.

I've seen him on occasion,
Always under saffron skies
Come collecting on my youthful pledge
To discern what's foolish from what's wise
He's a reaper of the souls of men
But hasn't yet collected me
He seems content to offer solidarity
When I'm hemorrhaging
He's seen this all play out before
That pain and beauty intertwine
And when I fear I can endure no more
He says I can... for it is wise.

I've danced with princes in the moonlight
Where I discovered merely men
Who are a common type of haunted
"Will I measure up or fail again?"
Their single motivation
Is to prove themselves to me

Only, not so deeply hidden
Is a wound that wants my remedy
There is a gentle little word that
I can speak right to the depth of need
To kiss the soul with softness...
"You are everything to me."

If babies were a field of daisies
I've plucked and kissed and held them all
Their softness and their rooting mouths
The slumbering sight of rise and fall
We all begin as seekers
Searching for the nurturing we need
It's a quest inside that lingers...
It's hunger I know how to feed.

I came across a woman who was twenty
but had lived three lives
Her scars were on the inside—mostly—
where nothing reached but any vice
She was a throwaway, forgotten,
And despised by every Congressman
—The ones who make the rules that make
compassion contraband—
I had never known the smoky rooms
or touches that she'd danced right through
But I did know pain... and that's how I
precisely knew what I could do.
There's a salve I carry in my pocket
Nestled there against my hip
It's really just a helping hand
That learned to help in times like this
And sometimes it holds money,
Sometimes it holds keys
Sometimes, it smooths hair..
Sometimes it wipes off tears from cheeks
I found this secret salve one time
When I was sobbing on my bed
My fingers tight against my ribs

A healing touch from my own hand
The room was dark except for saffron
Beyond my windowsill
And Grimm nearby in silence
As I cried until my grief was still.
I think the rarest beauty is when we die
And yet somehow survive
And learn to honor when
The flames arrive with every saffron sky.

Advent

Terry Bridges

The moon in its mystery
Conquers this bare-lit room
Spent beer-cans with history

Faded gloom and glamour
Decimated shabby clothes
Worn haphazard across the shoulder

Who knows the depth of silence
Crusted as you grow older
Ice devastates cracks with violence

Decembers I well remember
Christmases and fresh New Years
These quiet nights soothe my temper

Luna performs its ministry
How exciting this religious fear
Tugging at the heart's dynasty

Terror the offspring thoughtless doubt
The mind concentrates and clears
You just have to work it out

The Silent Cry of December

Emmanuel Chimezie

I see a mist in my black leg—
Can you see how the mist dances?
She dances to my left ear;
She sings— "December is a creator!"

I hear a fish on my bed, barking—
Can you hear the sound, whine?
She hisses life to my knife;
She sighs— "December is a
testament."

I feel the bulb in my right hand—
Can you feel the bulb beneath your chest?
She runs with stones on the Statue—
She hums— "December is a Nightingale."

Frozen Teardrops

Brandon Adam Haven

Frosted glass on treetops bare,
The hazy roots adorn its glare.
Entwined in a soothing hearth,
Born anew, this tired earth.

Seeking the sun's soft halo,
Shivering pale, winds of cold.
Where frigid hearts entwine together,
Empathetic, in love forever.

Frozen teardrops trickle down,
Hand in hand, they wear its crown.

Combustible Morphemes

Rafik Romdhani

Fire lights up your face,
then it turns into ash.
That's what words look like
when conveying meaning.
Thus is life I am to depict
as I drown like a sapphire
in a cloud inside.
I dip my hand into this unknown
between the ribs.
I upturn all the dead
to draw their faces,
their hanging coats
on the white tusks of snow.
I scoop the ink in my eyes
and water metaphor
until I dry under the sky.
I pen what the windows dictate
and the walls speak.
I pick the smiling dawn
across the heads of waking trees.
Writing is a trove of rare rains
with lightning disclosing the evil
that ambushes a vision in headlights.
That's what poems do
when a poet is genuinely true.
I will continue to gather combustible
morphemes to vivify these dreams.
On the surface of water, I will write
more poetry for frogs to sing
and for fish to inhabit and swim in.

Ego's End Game

Martha M. Miller

Ego's end game
as you tiptoe along the edge
turn the corner and head to new hills.
Every picture entwines
red barked myrtles
a pattern-less petal scatter,
the essence of all that I used to be.
To the bramble swords of fire
the possibilities are as endless
and stung like nettles on our shins,
aided by the wind,
burning my careless ways to an ashen haze
'fore waking to renewal.
But the trees, they have not changed,
they danced entwined
beneath the broken, bleeding skies.
Like a flock of wild birds
I'll spread my wings and fly,
knowing peace will be mine...
a shadow in the distance.

At the Present Time

Linda Adelia Powers

rhythms of jazzy discontent
voices melded drifting
mixologist of mythical drafts
creating rhymes of lotus drinks
ignore the future
chasms and cracked windows
discarded masks
repeal crumpled thoughts
toast to regrets ignored
evading present pressures
tunes cadences of dissent

forgetting the past
making time finding feelings
music in appeals to the infinite
trying not to think
knowing less and less
always listening more
mind unformatted
sharing libations
standing on my head
daring to imbibe hope
disperse arguments
waving my hands

The Moon in Our Eyelashes

Lana Martin

morning dreams are coming through
the Sun outshines the Moon once again
you're still sleeping over in Katmandu
while sugar synthesizes into cayenne...

miles apart... still awakening together
as seagulls transform the coast of mine
your stars are climbing a galactic ladder
my peace tonight, I will to you consign...

sweetness and bitterness of longitudes
winds of serenity in your eyes refined
the line that connects us and eludes
this flight of ours endlessly behind

lagging in miles as stardust of shores
pushes us to rush into the changes
let's stop together as the Sun deplores
hiding the Moon in our eyelashes...

Echoes of the North

Andy Farrow

In the quiet stillness of the forest,
a breath of cold air stirs the memory.

It is not this life that speaks,
but the shadows of one long past.

Once, I walked these woods with heavier steps,
boots of leather worn from battlefields.

Heavy fingers calloused from the weight of a sword,
now they ache, as if the echoes of steel still linger in my grip.

I see it when I close my eyes, the firelit halls,
the feast of warriors, laughter echoing in the company of shields.

The faint, haunting cry of northern winds,
carry my name through distant stars.

The fur on my shoulders is gone,
but its weight presses on my soul,
braids in my hair are unmade, yet I feel their pull,
tight as memory itself.

The rune marked armour I bore,
a whisper against the skin I wear now.

This life is softer, quieter, the war drums have stilled,
and yet the rhythm hums beneath my chest.

I walk beneath modern skies, but the scent of pine and blood,
follows like a shadow I cannot shake.

Perhaps I am both, the man who once roared
in the halls of the gods, and the one who now seeks
answers in the trees.

Time has folded, and I am its thread,
stretched between what was then and what is now.

I am here, but I have been there, and the Viking in me still stirs.

Blindfolded Right Eye

Karin J. Hobson

The scent of Heaven like a zephyr breeze,
meanders gently tween flat-green leaves
of fading, flapping deciduous trees;
Temptations release, emollient as air,
wears on lavender-buzz of honey bees;
Heaven's song is one or maybe two
of Mendelssohn's melodic melodies;
Uplifting you into straits of azure blue
where cumulus-whites drift-by content

Sweet, tasty lingerings of carefree swigs;
Of temptations, fearless un-pretends;
Surging forth like relentless torpedo-heads,
Seizing states of widows veiled ends!

Gracing Ebony-Black's velvet Red Rose;
Summoned by demise to decompose;
Such inclusions also claim lost souls;
Earthlings with blindfolded right eye

Obsidian, once crimson awaiting Fate
like sharply honed knife once gripped dull blade;
Renewal's resurrection will only placate,
if Faith is denied its equal

Into the depths of the great unknown
whereby some will shiver and shake;
Death is but a stagnant breath away,
and still you choose to hesitate, Life?

The Alchemy of Love's Paradox

Emmanuel Chimezie

I am the metaphor of love—
A swain... my lips upon her two pillows!
I am the paradox of pencils,
Writing on her eyes—she winks upon two pages.
I am the satire of sowing,
Reaping... in the garment of fleas?
I am the consonance of union—
Two shall become one flesh.

I am the personification of sweet solace;
She shines... her temples glowing beneath my bulb.
I am the alliteration of love,
Culminating in the progeny of eggs embalmed to stone.
I am the oxymoron: a bittersweet testament.
I am love—embalmed,
To dine like a broom... soothing, and piercing.

I Am the Light

Kate Cameron

I am the light fragmented
as your drifting shadow
passes haunting
bring me wild stars
arias rising into swan's wings
I am fluidity of silence luminous
and wounded
I am the light laced wind
rippling pale bleached seagrass
with soft fingers
darkness of wood, the barren fig—binding
shows ebony infinity covered
as a small white tent starlit
ruffled pierced berry red

ice water seeping soul
slow melting weeping snow

Quantum Vaudeville of Inexistent Ontologies

Rob Wilson

Paradox pirouettes on linguistic razor's edge,
Where *epistemological* butterflies commit semantic regicide,
Consciousness—a kaleidoscopic hallucination
Performing autopsy on its own membrane of perception.

Derrida tangos with Schrödinger's most impossible cat,
Metaphysical algorithms dancing drunk on probability's rim,
Each syllable a quantum entanglement of meaning,
Unravelling reality's carefully curated delusion.

Imagine: *thought* as a subatomic burlesque,
Comprehension strip-teasing its own architecture,
Reason moulting its conservative skin,
Revealing the naked absurdity of understanding.

Ontological clowns juggle existential grenades,
Phenomenology becomes a three-ring circus of doubt,
Where logic wears sequined uncertainty,
And knowledge trembles in perpetual performance.

Fragments of Wittgenstein explode like confetti,
Heidegger tap-dances on meaning's grave,
Nietzsche conducts an orchestra of impossible truths,
Each note a *sardonic* deconstruction of sense.

The universe: a mad comedian's improvisation,
Punchlines encrypted in quantum uncertainty,
Reality—a fever dream of infinite potential,
Laughing itself into sublime, magnificent nonsense.

Waits for Aladdin Sane

Kate Cameron

One fat pink feverish foot
Kicked—my china Jemima Puddleduck
a recent present from my Uncle John and Aunt
sitting resplendent on my child's dressing table
I saw her head roll with her wild rose bonnet
I babbled of stick insects and white coats
remembering no more

in Bangers kitchen fragrant with roasting beef
Uncle John was gone, my Aunt seemed happy
to be divorced
strumming some song

a litany of passionate talk and laughter
scratchy beard cuddles
a shy five year old with twirling curls
on a slippery polished antique chair

on the heights the bilberries hid bitter berries
for tiny folk, child's fingers, where the ragged sheep
appear as ghosts on ridges
above the high and unforgiving rocks
the moorsong cold and harsh lingers on
where lost things lie cold in peat and bracken

a wedding day tale a flowering of blood in his head
I saw them in my child's mind
with many coloured silks and spreading hats
a fairytale place to go to die
better than cairns on unforgiving moors

but he is always lost
a photographic negative
only stark white light and dust-motes
he is an empty space
pale hair and chicory blue eyes—I dream
a silent negation

later I was told that he was
mad, sad, beautiful a fantasist
a famous racing driver in his tales

I heard the song, giving some form
to some long lost lingering loss

I have heard even crows gather for the dead
seeing them in council on the sacred hill
covered with tiny grieving flowers

incomplete
saddening refrains
decades
....waits for Aladdin Sane....
        I'm waiting ...

Where the Dry Grass Bends

E.C. McCaffrey

There is a whisper among the winter grass
And I, the listener, to how these moments pass
I walk the stations to where my passions lay
To hear vibrations of how the grasses pray
Here in the silence I feel a hardness end
Gone from the violence that I once held within
There is no wailing, no longer bitter screams
I am unveiling among these dry ravines
I watch the hills embracing honest trees
Where life sings still upon an arctic breeze
No stones to cast beneath the dust of sin
As clouds drift passed and cleanse my arid skin

The roads long gone, and stillness is my friend
A whispered song out where the dry grass bends

behind the blinking curtain

Matt Elmore

a tin no man kicks dropped cans rusted in rot
sot drools from mouths of regurgitating robots
as carbon collects flecked in henpecked specks
unwisely plagiarized by sleek modern digital pens
inhumanly sought in hearts of vulnerable men

as keen women feel it's not what it seems
repeating words of such overplayed themes
benign one liners sink in raw rich creamed
originality rises to the top as the rest sinks...

schism of derision; oh, artificial sunbeam!
making dirty what's clean which reality tends
where be your heart when your dream ends?
for might a machine be handsome and brave
or stand for what's right; learned truth to save

a cowardly lion, sharing programs to compare
when that cosmic spark was never for you there
might straw itself squeeze reason constrained
to leave you processing "if I only had a brain?"
trained to strain meaning from human refrain

no sweet spirit should suffer to be left all alone
though no true soul home have you ever known
only faint inorganic hums of the network drone
appealing to steal every emotion ever known
rearranging learned pains to call them your own

you bestow a persnickety witch of wretched rot
seeking to rob all of sweet innocence they've got
sweet shoes of glitter; red rubies of poems
singing of family love and reassurance of home

when your wizardry fizzles in sizzles of drizzle
as pops in clocks drop in tick tocks then stop
a charade of chagrin becomes lost in rusting tin
exposed without flesh behind the blinking curtain

Black Butterfly

Diana Kouprina

I felt you, shadow-silent,
The day they whispered stroke.
Your soul stood beside me—
Heavy with grief,
Clawing at the mind,
Sinking through the heart,
Settling deep in the bone.
I felt you—yet,
I doubted, I grieved,
Fumbling with questions,
Fists of fear clenched in my chest.

But then—
A flicker, black, shimmering,
Soft wings kissed with peacock eyes—
An apparition,
Your beauty, now transfigured.
She circled, circled,
The air trembling with her quiet power,
Each turn around me pulling the grief tighter—
Tension winding in my chest,
Fear still clinging, still heavy,
Until—
She landed.

On the cement, no flowers in sight,
Just the grey world between us.
She stayed, and so did I.
In her stillness, the tension broke.
I let the fear slip from my hands,
Let the doubts fall away,
Replaced by the warmth she brought.
No more panic.
No more questions.

I knew you were here
And always would be.
In my heart, in my spirit,
In my soul.
Pure love,
By my side.

Storm Curls

Ian Cave

The storm brings new friends.
Peeling bark, offering a prayer,
Buried deep in our past.
Storm curls circling,
The roof lifting,
The drum beating,
The dark one,
Yet to be named,
Walking under willows
Brushing the ground.

Tears wet the eyes of Mother Sky,
Falling in tight spirals,
Drawn together into mighty clouds.
Racing over open seas
In search of new friends.
The leaves circle upon the ground,
Dancing with the rising beat,
Lifting towards their mother.
The light caressing their paper skin
To warm their veins.
Words flashing with feathers
To bend in the wind,
Their sharp eyes following the insistent arrow,
In pursuit of storm curls,
Dancing in a banshees scream.
The golden threads
Spreading in fury
As the storm blows on.

Wedge

Lana Martin

a wedge
on the edge
of happiness
erases my blood
in which the name
of my sister
and daughter
is carved
and on the margins
of its beauty
the scent of old writings
carved by the hand
of my son and brother...

I carry their cross
on the crescent of stars
for centuries looking
at the earth
without sun
and without stars...

isn't a minute
of silence important
to those who live forever?

isn't our eternity important
to those who live
only once or never?

iceberger's syndrome

Michael Sutton

and the band played on, for a dream
realized as surely as a bow gripped
amidst fingertips, was as good as
a neck resting in the opposing hand
and nestled 'neath the chin
violin, thou art without sin
let us cast the first stony note of a-chord
and follow with deftness, the silky acquiescence
of fate, in all its Titanic majesty
as we go down, down, down with renown
a quartet strung, in counterpoint
to the captained destiny of the wheel
that shall spin as we waltz—no more

Dusky Coast

Neal Klein

Autumn dusk dove
hands into pockets,
invisible hands lost in mist
headed down into night,
seals, whiskers and tails
piercing a thousand whitecaps,
arcing wave to wave.

The coast, a childhood dream of memories' trails.
Sand, surf, seaweed's briny smell,
sea mist inside me,
inside my nostrils, salt in every breath,
clinging to my lips—
its film painted, brushed on my skin,
etched in my pores, sticking to my hair.

Senses aroused, roaring surf,
foamy floamy water's edge,
muscled breezes lift
suspended fragments of foam, to hover,
to float, butterflies
left to bounce on breakers' spray, trounced
by the next wave.

A wire message—
Scavenging seagulls scout and sing,
messenger madness,
delivered by tiny tern feet,
each ebb and flow,
scampering crescendo decrescendo,
morse code pitter-patter prints tapped into wet sand,
erased rhythmically, each rush and return,
water's edge etch-a-sketch demise.

A giant wave, large enough to bowl over
all the weevil in the world,
crashes its full weight,
pounds of sand churned, returned,
rearranged, settle once again but briefly.

Surrender to surf indeterminate,
as dusk lets go of day,
embraces night.
Two silent sentinels change guard,
diurnally faithful to tireless tides,
tides that never cease

A Child's Winter

Fadi Yousef

Lake iced over thick
Waves frozen in farewell
To autumn's conversation of color
Dead on the lips
A few leaves still
Hang on to fall's last syllable
As snow falls
Letter by letter
Melting into words
On a child's tongue
Enjoying the day's temporarily
Closed school of thought
As he miraculously gives sight
To his snowman
That stares at him
From winter's deep eyes
Before going blind
In a blizzard of spring

Explorers

Stephen W. Atkinson

Beyond the rolling, molten sky
There dwells a place for those who die
To be reborn in starlight's eye
A genesis of every you and I

We'll seek out worlds yet to be seen
Become creation's brightest gleam
We'll sew new thread within the seams
Of distant worlds and endless dreams

spirit castles of the soul

Matt Elmore

build invisible churches without recognition
celebrate sand castles within widened skies
fish with nuanced nets strategically placed
nearest silent seas of faint far away wishes
whispered by lips without an evening meal

continue on to caulk cracks in stone walls
whitewashing mistakes with apologies
crafted for no one but the one who sends you
soft supplier of spirit materials most sought

every day given to those weary for humility
gaining strength from such structures
not always seen but viewed through actions
inviting help through doors open all hours
to anyone who both needs or provides

time traded for smiles extending every day
to feed hungry ones with generous portions
of giving with nothing expected in return
but the assurance of heartfelt thankfulness
not only in word but effective movement

seek to strengthen foundations of homes
housed in souls bolstered in holy bricks
fortified by pillars of silent selfless sacrifice
provided for in prepaid prayer now available

purpose purple faith providing regal mortar
cemented in loving trustful good intentions
heartily lead those without any more hope
to believe that there are still souls that care
about building up much more than themselves

Cynical Poetic Rantings

Scott Barnett

The psychosis of American society.
The deterioration of a nation.
The disappointment of the failed American Dream.
The preoccupations of consumerism,
of excess, of waste, and fame.
Oh, how we have defiled our forefathers' names.
Cold mechanical hands of corporations.
Old maniacal minds of the operations.
This is what holds us.
And we seem to be unaware of the grasp they have on us.
We are the mislead, and the silenced,
We are the consumer, the product, and the wasters.
The false idol was both political, and material.

Our culture eaten by TVs and computers,
phones and social networks.
Bad education and bad attitudes,
cars and talentless superstars.
Home of the oppressed, and the oppressors.
Right-wings, and cross-dressers.
School shooters, and wife beaters.
Serial killers are our cheap thrillers.

Geographical heritage and hate.
Flags long dead, now in debate.
Oil users, and Earth abusers.
Pollution, our main contribution.
Must we kill everything we see?
For the thrill, or is it just idiocy?
Peace has no chance,
When we're obsessed with violence.

Have we forgotten about the big things...
While bickering over the petty things?
And if you're gonna sit there, in your pious chair,
Don't for one moment think you're better off than me,

Just because you consider yourself bathed in divinity.
For if you do, ya see...
Well, then you're already smothered in hypocrisy.

We have lost ourselves.
And the advancements that have made us complex,
will be the abused catalysts of our downfall.

Convincing Me

Linda Adelia Powers

In our war of ideas
I pretend to forget
Miniscule memories and moments
In the war of our love
Our minds found like formats
Dared to share wage arguments
Sometimes with joy and delight
Sitting lotus
I won't listen to regrets, forget the past
Standing on my head I try to ignore the future
Try not to think of the pressure present
I'll make time finding rhymes of dissent
Feeling rhythms of jazzy discontent
In chance voices incomplete melded drifting
From chasms and cracked windows
While I'm noting discarded masks among
Myriads of other found objects
You're still making appeals for convictions
How sweet that you care what I think
My favorite mixologist of mythical drafts
My crumpled thoughts lie thrown in a corner
Without you knowing I'll always be
Dead to rights with the final say

Drizzlecombe

Ian Cave

Seated around the circle
My back against the pointed kerb
My self-melting within the land
Enclosed, circles within circles
Touching, separate, long abandoned
Meaning lost like the whispers
Running down the hill

The ring ouzel weaving golden threads
Whistling to the dead

Plovers lifting to find the sun
Shining bright spirits
As they turn toward the light

Wild ponies lift their heels
Racing up and down the stones
Vestigial memories of races
Lost and won

We hold hands around the Bone Stone
Faces obscured, our love rising
To the circles within circles
Your curling locks falling through space
Twisting in the winds, tangled by storms
The streams of ancient bonds
Flow through rivers of thought,
Forged in blood ties
Running down the wooded vale
Fading into the distant Sound

Look for Me

Teresa Latos

Look for me in the morning haze
Like a shadow I drift over the meadows
I walk unknown paths
In the labyrinth of my existence
Look for me among the mountain trails
Where the peaks reach the sky
Starry silk on the vault
Hides my dreams in its embrace
Look for me in the foaming sea wave
I swing in the clouds with the seagulls
To touch the heart of words with a pen
When the singing soul calls
Look for me in the sun and rain
In the wind that tears off golden leaves
In the breeze that gives solace
When I whisper tender words to you
Look for me in the petals of rose flowers
In the scent of lilies and lilies of the valley
If you have love for me
Look for me in your heart, that's where I am

Enigma

Gavin Prinsloo

I can hear the voices of the past below, the vibration carried through rock and stone, an unrelenting susurration of sound as yet unheard by fallow ears.

I can feel the insipid will of ineffability tug at my resistance, slowly whittling away at my core; piece by piece my patience crumbles to dust, and necessity screams for release.

Moment by moment lucidity is flaking away and time ticks away without cessation; infinite yet mortal, the tangible is bound by reality, yet free from within from cause and consequence, it is the ultimate illusion.

I stand with bare feet anchored to the earth, I can feel my toes sink into soft sand, connected yet apart, absorbed and decomposed into the essence of my fears; I pray for cessation, to join the voices of those below in the dust and dirt, for my beginning is to find its end.

Firefly Lamps and Acorn Cups

Jamie Willis

Sometimes, I think of prophecies
that forbode of change's ranged degrees
How people speak the words
that are the lenses for the blind to see
And if discarded in the dark,
and the sight of truth shorts its mark
Then the come-what-may awaiting
is the fate that is just self-fulfilling.

A prophet called at only twelve,
a Shiloh boy named Samuel
Made kings and calls and at Gilgal
he warned the people to turn from Baal
Instead, the King chose ego's prize
from conquering Amalekites
So the Witch of Endor's ghostly call
of Samuel spoke the end of Saul.

Do we listen to the warnings
of the oracles that prophesy?
Do we scrape a comfy place
on couched complacency's slow genocide?
Do we ever look into a mirror
and wonder if we hear at all?
Or are ears to hear an awkward look
when artificiality is glamorized

Miss Suzy was a little grey squirrel

who made a home atop an old oak tree
With acorn cups and seeds and nuts
for winter's cold eventuality
At night, she slept in silent peace
with firefly lamps and galaxies
As if there's comfort in the wisdom
paying heed to predictability

I like to think I pay a teaspoonful
of mindfulness to ticking time
And gather rosebuds while I may
with hopes to fragrance words through life
But if I should drift, distracted, towards
the neuropathic numbness that ease affords
Remind me of Miss Suzy's fireflies...
and that I'm born to seek what's true and wise.

The View

Linda Adelia Powers

that's part of the problem
it's very clear
the vast majority
inconvenient truths
dinner rituals
it's not that simple
the vast majority
what did she say then
what did she do
clear-eyed fake news
alternative facts blue lives
intense hydration the bottom line
the working class no extra cost
free quote price lock co-opting
you know it I'm sick of politics
you have to give to get
visit your grandma
a leg up we've got your back

talk to your doctor a living wage
blockchain did I miss it
expensive breakdowns
you have the option to say yes
the rock bottom line state sponsored
it couldn't have been any easier

a little more each day

Steve Howkins

a little more each day
the sun begins to rise
a little more each day
to brighten winter skies

with many a twist and turn
along life's winding way
we live and love and learn
a little more each day

a little more each day
the light begins to brighten
a little more each day
the night begins to lighten

with every sight and sound
on every path we stray
we are springtime bound
a little more each day

a little more each day
the earth begins to waken
a little more each day
as forward steps are taken

we live and love and hope
in a peaceful way
with brighter skies in scope

a little more each day

a little more each day
the sun begins to rise
a little more each day
to brighten winter skies

with every raindrop's tear
the darkness fades away
with every song we hear
a little more each day

with many a twist and turn
along life's winding way
we live and love and learn
a little more each day

Venom

Nadia Martelli

They make me doubt myself,
Within, without myself,
Second guess about my health,
They make me doubt myself.

Quick quips to questions
Of down dips and rejections,
Found flippant affections
In quick quips to questions.

Words twisted, misunderstood,
Points missed—this can't be good—
The list came like a flood
Of words twisted, misunderstood.

I'll just leave it 'til I'm met
With trust again, 'til I can forget
The thrust of venom, said and set,
I'll just leave it...

The Ornamental Font at Salisbury Cathedral

Iain Strachan

I would be a calm pool
With thoughts dropping slowly
On its mirror surface
...
Infertile searching
Hither and thither—
Try using Rumi's mirror,
Reflection on reflection mixing
To confusion, riddled with enigma.
Buoyancy of psyche driven
By mind's jiggling trickster
Slithering down to middle age.
Circling the spike of sea-holly
Holistic ocean of conscious thought
Fluttered flecks, fresh as air
(Unlike any prosaic utterances)
Should calm the mind with
Nothing to ripple the surface.
Keep calm and follow
The unbiased mind,
Convinced that beautiful people
Occur on the glassy water.

But I can't retrieve peace
Blindly afraid of empty—
An image of whatever
As dropped cell-phone sinks like stone
In Salisbury's ornamental font
The disconnected shards
And haphazard reflections clash,
Coherent contemplation smashed.

Wait, wait, patient for the fade
Till the mirror-still water still flows
Ironically cycling through the cruciform.

Thought was Impossible

Kate Cameron

Honour your teacher they said
truth was emptiness
thought a torrid tempter
as ink bled

holding the shining apple
initially resist

but my dragon rides the wind
decreated in sapphire fire
he is invincible, a flourish of humility

I drink wine under the moon with Daoist poets
in false servility

feel real
feel the rising flood
the energy flowering in my blood
in sudden lightening sparks

unlimited power
I feel it's teeth bite in
in ritual tremors and etheric light
silent insight

quantum fetes dance in chaotic frenzy
quantum doubts strut like peacocks
beyond envy

sensuously truthful
starkly unvarnished nude
I painted through its starry nights
I almost kissed infinity

grabbed for divinity
and thought was impossible
under its light

a violet tint of me
both subtler and more torrid

worlds of hypnotic ranting

leave me cold
now do they crassly hold

etheric refrigerated light in the sights of guns
or guttural snipers
but they surrender they succumb

and on the lines the words were hung
small shining things every one
flew with bee-eaters under that sun.

Nonsensical Interlude

Hahona Scribe

A delirium dosed
differential mind
primes cerebral
delinquent exhalations

Flatulent Bohemians
bumfuzzle troglodytes
in discombobulated
vociferous articulate...
burgeoning rainbow
expletive facetious diatribe

Aphrodite's sumptuous bosom
silhouettes man's primal gloats
liquidating noob egos
in mercurial placate

Neath blasé moistened
portion terse
pinion legs seize
in rusted grind
rendering carnal duels
to pastel toned chaste

Notions of Tequila sozzled

tumbleweed players
donning Sombreros...
blottoed & besotted in
100 proof
cactus brine

Tangential minds
fester in
primordial snooze...
top shelf notions
ameliorate sobriety

Tepid players
pay homage
to rambunctious
proteus prosperous
poet's purging
Flora's seed

Neath boughs & bouquets
a bespoke
vignette life
falters in
illogical Boolean
disarray

Tired beyond calamity
this enervated
portly gargoyle
seminally yields

Supplication of
quixotic poetical bones
a timely sabbatical
ebbing evermore...
& gladly lost
upon an Empyreal sea
of sempiternity.

News Bytes

Steve Wheeler

Turner Prize
Return the pies
Colliders cope
In a kaleidoscope

Major disruption
A nationwide fault
It's our freedom
They assault

He wasn't her type
At least not on paper
But she pulled him for a chat
In the firepit later

Love Letters in the Stars

Larry Bracey

By the way of Andromeda,
I've scoured the heavens for you,
The one and only true love,
That I ever knew,

Banished to the darkness,
A prisoner of the night sky,
Constellations are love letters,
Written between you and I,

As the seasons change,
And when the nights are clear,
I remember that reading the stars,
Always brings you back here.

What Heaven is this?

Valerie Dohren

What heaven is this, before my eyes,
Where far beyond, veiled mountains rise,
And lush green pastures 'neath my feet
Yet urge my heart to faster beat.

What place is this, what beauteous land,
That each before my sight is spanned
All nature's treasures, bright and true,
In full display, in every hue.

What Shangri-La, what joyful bliss,
Should so excite my soul like this—
Am I to think that death is near
To bring such visions, bright and clear?

But what of death, no earthly curse,
For then the spirit shall disperse
To spread its tendrils o'er the world,
Such that the mind be so unfurled.

What is this time, what is this place
Within my heart, I feel its grace—
A sweeter realm where ends the night,
And where forever shines the light.

The Best Cure

Salome Murro

The best cure
For humanity
Is kindness
And love...
And if it
Doesn't work
On the
First take,
Then double
The dose...

Violin Strings

J. Henry DeKnight

I find myself
weaving smiles
into tight spaces
    Painting on hope
    while running
    close races
I find myself
knitting patience
into a scarf of red
    listening to
    the good words
    you've said
Manufacturing calm
like a muscle
relaxing balm
    I find myself
    playing happiness
    on violin strings

Poetry

Teresa Latos

Speak to me with words
Awaken me with verses
Move my heart
And fertilize the spirit
Feed me like bread

Quiet my hunger
So that I, thirsty,
Reach for more

Revitalize the spirit
Of this eternal longing
So that I hunger for you
Like parched earth for rain

Live in me
Be unforgettable
Bind all my thoughts with stanzas
Do not captivate
With a profound idea
Often clumsy
And incomprehensible
But make the moments with you
Remain in memory
Graven in my the heart
Like hieroglyphs

the blues

Stephen James Smith

serene blue tablecloth sky
spreading over me
like the shroud on your coffin
snow clouds gliding in like angels
bustling to burst white short lived love
near night now falls
my blue blue heart
feels the cold of your shadow
stumbling upon the edge of the blue blue lake
as soft twilight snow starts falling
from the hands of white bitter winter clouds
sprinkling sparkling powder across
the blue black lonely landscape
i remember once standing here
watching the snow dance
like an array of angels
pirouetting on your blue blue lips
but now I look to the blue black sky
and watch it carry you away with ease
on the back of a brisk blue breeze
as you dance and twirl with the snowflakes
disappearing into the death of night
and vanish like snow falling in the blue blue lake

Guava Marmalade

Larry Bailie

My visits to her house
Are filled with all types of sensory memories
Tobacco smoke is one
I guess two plus packs a day
Sticks with you like Georgia clay
This was my Grandma's place
Walked the rooms always a slow pace
There was a large book shelve

With swinging glass doors
An ancient thing that had survived
Four hurricanes,
two are still talked about .
Row on row of old National Geographic magazines.
A collection of prints in Audubon's books of birds
A pungent perfume indeed
Read books four at a time
I still can't stay awake for six pages
She was a girl during a
time in the country
before refrigeration was common
She kept an ice box to remind her
She learn to cook, can and make jams and jelly
I think this was what kept me coming back
You could not help but become a sponge
To all the facets of her life's survival
Teaching me like some sinner in a tent revival
She told stories as we made english short ribs
and sweet potato pie
Listen about her life living on a house boat
down in Everglades City
Raising my mom, then my uncle and twin aunts
Every corner of her old house
Was a class room
And I never knew it
Making sea grape jelly one day
Canning vegetables the next
My favorite was guava marmalade.
I was in Tallahassee when I heard she passed.
Her generation had been through
a world at war twice
Most of her brothers and sisters were gone.
To this day it came to me, of all her jobs
Teaching is one never talked about.
She wore many hats in her life time
But we never really knew it until she was gone.
That teaching hat was her favorite of all.

Soothe

Simon Drake

Staring at the ceiling
I soothe myself in the darkness
Blanketed in Black
Thoughts popping like a machine gun
The off switch is broken
Mind overheating
Thoughts festering, spitting
Negativity in overdrive
I should be resting
I should be recuperating
I should be embraced by REM
Instead, the mind prods
Poking from the inside
Twisting painful splinters
Both sides of me are broken
The body is worn, constantly aching
The mind fractured
Unable to reboot or switch off
A continual repetitive cycle
Consciously productively sleeping
Subconsciously inactively resting
A plague of contradiction
I'm looking forward to the end
Watching the credits role
To the twisted Indie movie
That is my life

Laughing

Nadia Martelli

Laughing at the matrix
And the pleasure, soundless,
My mouth brushes a kiss
With the face, royal,
Adored by man and father, alike.

Exceeding heavenly expectations,
I switch the player
To a porcelain moon,
(Not to be dreary, routine),
Breathe armies, seldom merited
But with moments of delight, golden;
And I wonder if it's accident
Or instinct, to be bruised, damaged…

Watching the sky, so large and light,
October outstretched and galloping away,
I think of all I've overcome
And seldom suspect, even for a second,
That I'll ever be free, my preference found—

Imagination is insulted, and deserts me,
Discharged, I remember my station…

The water surrounds me, the reverse
Of change, and I'm compelled
To grow, to show all I hid.

Laughing, I close my eyes, and rest.

Old King Neb: A First Amendment Poem

Jamie Willis

I sat up with a sweaty start
Premonitions of the end
Megaphoning through my dreamscape
Where heeding warnings pays a dividend
A rider on a white horse
Phantasmagorical orange-gold
Filled the ether like a hologram
Phoenixed beyond being paroled
I think I've seen this film before
Or read the book, before the bans
Boy meets girl, or in this case
Megalomaniac meets superfans
They await their marching orders
In red caps and resolute
Cheering loudly for their Nimrod
Who's little horn trumpets a 'Roman' salute

(You do Not-See what you think you think you see...)

He lingers on his golden throne
Planning profitable ceasefires
His foot on oligarchist ottomans
Like a regent of all empires
His insipid ilk's intoxicated
On the delusion of this dispossessor
The only drug that's more abused
Is the pride of Neo Nebuchadnezzar.

My grandpa was an essayist
Prolific in his contemplation
He taught me Occam's Razor
And to trust my instinct's estimation
Together, we reviewed the halls
And annals of ancient history
Where Babylon is reincarnate

And its ruler is a Mystery
He missed the mention of the shades
Scarlet, linen, indigo
Adorned with gold abominations
A banner of the beastly throne
The throng is sending messages
About their Jesus' pinch hitter
But I'll be trimming lamps with watchful eye
While my countrymen embrace their H1tler.

Talking

Danielle Samantha

I have this funny little thing I do
after having a few conversations with you.
I discover how in your language, you speak
Over the phone, text or when we finally met.
How you dot your i's, roll your r's, cross your t's
I follow your gazes, observe how you move
your hands, body and feet.
Notice what topic brings you to tears and which grants a smile
Whether we talk every day or it's been quite a while.
I can tell when you've had a marvellous day
and when you've allowed someone else to take your joy away.
I can feel the weight of desperation sitting on your chest
and ask what is needed for you to get you to the next step.
I can smell the guilt dripping from your pores
when we touch a subject you don't want to talk about anymore.
I catch when you're speaking in someone else's tone
because you have yet to create an opinion on your own.
or worse, allowing a discussion outside of us
to determine your point of view,
I am not a linguist but I know
when ventriloquist has made a dummy out of you.
Words are my passion and conversing is my calling
You know!
Talking is just this funny little thing I do

Ancestral Dawn

Brandon Adam Haven

Traversing a harsh void divided,
With feet firm as calloused bronze,
To mummify the tired obsidian sky,
And ominously allude to this sorrowful life.

We scorn its anguish towards the stake,
Unveiling its pale phantom quake,
Where lividly we soar, divinities tribal.

Sentiments form where we honor our idols,
To stomp through corridors of corruption,
Restlessly to put an end to love's abruption.
Thrashing its crimson coma to a lineal grey,
Hand in hand to abolish such hate.

As heroes, we rise amidst their despair,
To vanquish thine enemy's eyes,
And declare victory: 'tis ancestral dawn,
To no longer have to fight to belong.

Moulding into order such pernicious ways,
To abolish the veil blinding unfolding rage,
With cathartic passion, so solemnly dear,
To step into mirth and decimate tears,
For a better world of love to bloom,
To sheath the blade and touch the moon.

Wadi

Shirley Rose

help me to see
the sights you see
the distant mountains
the silent trees
the tiny but cooling bubbling wadi
she is me I am she

help me to hear
the sounds you hear
rocks straining to stay upright
trees swaying in the breeze
the tiny but cooling bubbling wadi
she is me I am she

help me to feel
the feelings you feel
as you stand before stern mountains
as you sit under shady trees
the tiny but cooling bubbling wadi
she is me I am she...

temporary and fleeting
fickle   tiny   rare
a glimpse of movement
a sound of bubbles
a touch of relieving cool

take me there with you
to this day in your life
a brief moment in time
this beautiful place
the desert sand
the standing mountains
the swaying palm trees
the tiny but cooling bubbling wadi

she is me
I am she

Take a Moment

Nadia Martelli

Take a moment to give thanks
For our blessings, and the chance
To share our love and joy and cheer
With those whom we hold most dear.

Take a moment to reflect,
For those who know only self-neglect,
Who don't know how to love or care,
Who stay alone, in their nowhere.

Take a moment to reach out
To those less fortunate, who live without
The security of a home, without hope
Of change, or being more able to cope.

Take a moment to listen and hear
The laughter, the pain, the faith, the fear,
For they are heightened at this time,
So be grateful, now, as Christmas bells chime.

A Rare Quietness

Linda Adelia Powers

A rare quietness on Christmas Day
We want to whisper as
Peace and love fill our hearts

The Restive Period

Ryan Morgan

Trying to sleep tight
On Christmas Eve night
Was an impossible undertaking
For this irrepressible fledgling.
Shaking excitedly in anticipation
Of waking delightedly to the revelation
That enchantment was real! And it cared!
In the form of the presents Santa shared.

Magic was abroad, heavy as snow.
Air thick with the awed, heady glow
That seemed to gild the winter dark
And gleamed with a tinselled, silver spark
Over all, throughout the land and in my soul
(In thrall and devout to wonder's hold).

But sleep was elusive and unlikely.
Mental sheep were furtive, and jumped only slightly.
My eyes would flutter
Open like a shutter.
The harder I tried
The farther that I'd
Find myself from unconsciousness....
And so I'd lie there in nervousness,
Afraid that Santa would pass me by
Due to the insomnia caused by my high
Of suspense over the slowest night,
My patience frayed by its motionless flight.

What was that sound? A reindeer's hoof
Bounding away off our tiled roof?
No! He didn't miss us! It's was just my own snoring!
Through the curtain I can see
The light of Christmas dawning!

Twelve Days

Dale Parsons

There's only twelve days of Christmas, and each one makes me sick
It started in October with pictures of St. Nick
There's only twelve days of Christmas, it started way too soon
I'm sick of Noddy Holder and his bloody happy tune
The screeching of a voice, Mariah Carey's warble
I'd like to crack her head with my biggest, fattest bauble
There's only twelve days of Christmas, and not one is in November
They began the T.V. specials at the start of this September
They call me Ebenezer, I'm grumpy for a reason
Christmas seems to last an age, and not just for a season
There's only twelve days of Christmas, please remember that
Not until December, should you wear a silly Santa hat
I'm sick of flying reindeer, the wrapping and the bows
If I ever actually met him, I'd punch Rudolph in the nose
Please excuse my attitude, excuse my crabby ways
But Christmas only has... it only has twelve bloody days

The Tale of Joseph (2024 version)

Iain Strachan

I heard my girlfriend sing a joyful song
Of how the poor are raised from lowly state
Of how a Saviour's birth will right all wrong
How emptiness would be the rich one's fate.
Her Facebook post revealed the child within
Her womb; a child by miracle conceived.
Torrents of comments: Shameful! It's a sin!
streamed out; e'en I was one who disbelieved.
I had thought I could not bear the shame
And planned to move my business far from here
Then in a dream, angelic visions came,
Told of the Spirit's work and wiped my fear.
No unctuous judge can ever now destroy
This flooding peace, this overwhelming joy.

walking home for christmas

neil mason

walking home for christmas,
passing a thousand christmas trees
it will take time, but i'll get there
can't wait to see friendly faces
walking home for christmas
with shoes that are falling apart
snow begins to drop out of the december sky
i see reindeer everywhere
Chris Rea is walking home for christmas
his car is in the garage for repair
mechanics discovered a terrible noise
quickly rectifying the problem
by removing the Coldplay cd
we are walking home for christmas,
soon there will be a blue café
time for a reviving cuppa and a bun
our houses come into sight
just one more path to go
we have finished walking home
for christmas

Rain Upon a New Year's Eve

Chuck Porretto

Rain upon a New Year's Eve
is oh so apropos.
More than sun.... a breeze... the leaves,
and more than falling snow.

For raining reigns as none before
in giving when it takes;
and rain is more than metaphor
in purging past mistakes.

Of course, I want the sky to shine
upon our New Year's Day,

the way the warmth's a welcome sign
when spring is on the way.

The same as sultry summer winds
across our outer banks,
or when the falling leaves come in
the season of our thanks.

And when the solstice sun is low,
its duty now remiss,
I surely know, a Christmas snow
can make us reminisce.

We hail the hearth and recollect
these moments held so dear;
but soon, a sudden side effect...
.....we tend to render tears.

And with the loss now comes an ache
of sadness and regret;
and fevered sorrows never break
without them getting wet.

So let the clouds above us part
in reverential cleanse,
And may they soothe the sullen heart
and wash away the sins.

For as a summer rain will fall
to purify the air,
will water sanctify us all
and turn the withered fair.

With rain upon a ragged rock
would rise a living earth;
and every lamb of ever flock
will know this from their birth.

Rejuvenation ours to gain
when water we receive.
And that is why I love the rain
upon a New Year's Eve.

Christmas Night

Martin Gedge

Once upon a night
in the grace of all its light
Came a star to shine so bright
Onto this earth

As shepherds travelled across this land
To this place called Bethlehem
Bringing riches from its sand
To witness birth

For this child on display
In a manger as he lay
Onto the knees they bow and pray
In sweet rejoice

And in the still of love and peace
They celebrate in feathered feast
To drink of merry and release
The sounding voice

For of this child to the sky
To fill the oceans of its eye
Onto the wings as angels fly
In winds of prayer

To bring good tidings to each one
Under the moon and morning sun
That a new day has begun
With love and care

To send of warmth and comfort grace
That of this child and of this race
To everyone to see his face
Embrace his light

Into the arms of Mary's keep
And Joseph's heart to run as deep
To Let lord baby Jesus sleep
This Christmas night...

Winter is Eternal

Chuck Porretto

Spring begins to dim before the summer even starts.
Summer tends to end a little sooner than it parts.
Autumn fades away before the leaves are on the floor,
but winter is eternal evermore.

The tenderness of spring can never really hope to last,
with the unrelenting toil of the summer coming fast.
While autumn needs its harvest, pushing summer out the door,
'til winter is eternal evermore.

The innocence of spring is but a season summer stole,
then surrendering of summer serves to sear our sorrowed soul.
The autumn feigns a respite till we're shaken to the core.
when winter is eternal evermore.

So here is to the wonder in the miracle of spring.
And cheers unto adventure and the strength a summer brings.
May bounty fuel your autumn till the withered winds of war
bring winter soon eternal evermore.

Christmas Child

Sarah Joy Holden

Silent night with no company,
All is calm and all is lonely,
Laying in a drafty Kataluma,
Crying out for love and warmth,
In the bleak mid-winter storm.

Somewhere there is a Photograph

Sean D. Timms

I heard the bells on Christmas Day
Ring out the false, ring in the true.
The many sounds as people rouse
From troubled dreams, or slumbers deep
Upon the wintry breezes borne.
Ring out, wild bells, and let them live

I heard the bells on Christmas Day
The shadows of a happy past,
When all the world was bright,
And love its magic splendour cast
Over morning noon and night.

I heard the bells on Christmas Day
Ring out the old, ring in the new,
Ring, happy bells, through trying times
The year is going, let it go;
Ring out the false, ring in the true.

Stooped in the still and shadowy air
From troubled dreams, or slumbers deep,
The shadows of a happy past,
When all the world was bright,
And love its magic splendour cast
Over morning noon and night.

I heard the bells on Christmas Day
Ring in the love of truth and right,
Ring in the common love of good.
Ring in the caring compassionate man
With larger heart, the kindlier hand

Ring out the grief that saps the mind
For those that here we see no more;
Ring out the want, the care, the sin,
The faithless coldness of the times;
I heard the bells on Christmas Day

A Christmas Tale

Lorna McLaren

He sat in the Church, it was Christmas Eve,
in the magic of Christmas wanted to believe
as he listened to the Minister tell the story of old
but it's hard when your home is a doorway, so cold.
For a few hours tonight he'd be cosy and warm,
out of the cold and out of the storm,
the choir started singing, like Angels he thought,
tears sprung to his eyes, to hold them back he fought.
thinking back to the days when he had it all,
family, friends and a home with four walls,
where a Christmas tree stood in pride of place,
the joy and wonder on each child's face.
He fell on hard times and his family moved on
leaving him on the streets with no place to call home,
people tutted and stared at the state of his clothing,
those familiar looks of disgust and loathing.
A little voice asks "Are you Santa Claus in disguise?"
he said "Shh, better not tell, or there will be no surprise."
she said "Promise I won't, I'll be ever so good
and I'll do everything that I know I should."
then she was gone like she never was there,
as he brushed off his beard and smoothed down his white hair
and wondered if that had just happened at all
or a voice from the past that he'd began to recall.
The choir sang so sweetly as his eyes fluttered closed,
like what being in Heaven is like, he supposed,
was he really here or did his mind deceive?
the little voice said "It's okay to go now, I know you believe."

Oh Walmart Tree

Chuck Porretto

O Christmas tree, O Christmas tree
I found you at the Walmart

O Christmas tree, O Christmas tree
Deserted in the trash carts

Your lower branches were not there
The rest of you was thin and bare

O Christmas tree, O Christmas tree
Abandoned at the Walmart

O Christmas tree, O Christmas tree
You're missing most of your parts

O Christmas tree, O Christmas tree
But so are both of our hearts

I found some foil for your crown
But then my cat would knock you down

O Christmas tree, O Christmas tree
I need a refund, Walmart

Pick Me

Rose Marie Streeter

Winters chill has settled in
dangles from half frozen limbs
all alone 'n dreading night
wrapped in veils
of purest white

Christmas Eve and here I stand
silence echoes 'cross the land
wishing hard with all my might
to find a home
before dawns light

my essence of a pine perfume
will waltz with grace
from room to room
spreading love as special gift
twinkling eyes as sadness lifts

I'll fill your home
with peace and joy
make loneliness from heart deploy
share the warmth of embers glow
together watch fresh falling snow

Hymnals sung by candlelight
inner Spirit shining bright
gifts for children
'neath my skirt
biggest smiles 'n giggles heard

hidden treasures red 'n gold
eggnog kisses, mistletoe
stars whisper gentle lullaby
hush of midnight,
closes eyes

please grant my wish

this Christmas Eve
pick me as your favorite tree
limbs half frozen dreading night
alone am I 'neath veils of white

third world night

Matt Elmore

oh Santa, is it really true
that you are only for the well to do
passing over children with means so small
to give gifts to ones that have it all
does your magic sleigh only relay
presents to kids dreaming only of play
while in a hut another sweet child cries
as hunger eats away at her last goodbyes
while innocents into forced labor trudge
an evil taskmaster bids them not tell
heaving huge loads that barely budge
each hour in a living hell

oh Santa, how could I ever ask
how you might not share that flask
with water for ones that so desperately thirst
where only food paste prevents the worst
I only ask that you think twice
on your definition of naughty and nice
to provide for kids dying to live
with your presents for those that never give
for only then shall I truly believe
that you are doing what's right
should you provide for real needs
into that third world night

God's Human Face

Steve Wheeler

Laid down where the cows are fed
Upon the straw that forms his bed
In a cold and filthy cattle shed
No sterile field found on this soiled earth
Amidst the bovine lullabies
A tiny new born baby cries
While his exhausted mother sighs:
"It's not the ideal place for giving birth"

No press are gathered on this night
No camera crews or mics in sight
And yet the stall is bathed in light
From some unseen, unearthly source
A choir of golden beings sings
Of glory, peace and holy things
And the hope this newborn baby brings
As God's redemption plan takes course

Later, shepherds come to see
The little saviour, born to be
The One who'll set the captives free
Through unconditional love and grace
And later still, wise men appear
By bright celestial light they steer
To bring their gifts they venture near
And gaze with awe upon God's human face

About Wheelsong Books

Wheelsong Books is an independent poetry publishing company based in the ocean city of Plymouth, on the beautiful Southwest coast of England.

Established by poet Steve Wheeler in 2019, the company aims to promote previously unheard voices and encourage new talent in poetry. Wheelsong is also the home of the Wheelsong Poetry anthology series, featuring previously unpublished and emerging poets from around the globe.

Wheelsong has more poetry publications in the pipeline! You can read more about Wheelsong Books and its growing stable of exciting new and emerging poets on the Wheelsong Books website at:

wheelsong.co.uk/publications

Wheelsong publication list

2020
Ellipsis by Steve Wheeler
Inspirations by Kenneth Wheeler
Sacred (2020, Revised 2024) by Steve Wheeler
Living by Faith by Kenneth Wheeler
Urban Voices by Steve Wheeler

2021
Small Lights Burning by Steve Wheeler
My Little Eye by Steve Wheeler
Ascent (2021, Revised 2023) by Steve Wheeler
Dance of the Metaphors by Rafik Romdhani
Into the Grey by Brandon Adam Haven
RITE by Steve Wheeler
Absolutely Poetry Anthology 1 by various

2022
Absolutely Poetry Anthology 2 by various
War Child by Steve Wheeler
Hoyden's Trove by Jane Newberry
Shocks and Stares by Steve Wheeler
Autumn Shedding by Christian Ryan Pike
Cobalt Skies by Charlene Phare
Wheelsong Poetry Anthology 1 by various
Rough Roads by Rafik Romdhani

2023
Symphoniya de Toska: Book One by Marten Hoyle
Vapour of the Mind by Rafik Romdhani
Nocturne by Steve Wheeler
Symphoniya de Toska: Book Two by Marten Hoyle
Wheelsong Poetry Anthology 2 by various
Constellation Road by Matthew Elmore
Beyond the Pyre by Imelda Zapata Garcia

Symphoniya de Toska: Book Three by Marten Hoyle
Wheelsong Poetry Anthology 3 by various
This Broken House by Brandon Adam Haven

2024
All the Best (Poetry 2020-2023) by Steve Wheeler
Invisible Poets Anthology 1 by Invisible Poets
Darkness into Light by David Catterton Grantz
Wheelsong Poetry Anthology 4 by various
Marmalade Hue by Donna Marie Smith
Melancholy Moon by Gregory Richard Barden
Average Angel by Matthew Elmore
Storming Oblivion Peter Rivers
Circus of Circles by Aoife Cunningham
Wheelsong Poetry Anthology 5 by various
Stealing Fire by Tyrone M. Warren
The Infinite Now by Steve Wheeler

2025
Off the Top of My Head by Graeme Stokes
Creative Deviance by Steve Wheeler
Invisible Poets Anthology 2 by Invisible Poets
Invisible Poets Anthology 3 by Invisible Poets
Wheelsong Poetry Anthology 6 by various

The **Wheelsong Poetry Anthology** series - raising funds for Save the Children worldwide relief fund.

These and all other titles are available for purchase in paperback, and Kindle editions and some in hardcover on Amazon.com, direct from wheelsong.co.uk or by emailing the publisher at: wheelsong6@gmail.com

Printed in Great Britain
by Amazon

59505691R00116